Re-Introducing Christianity

Re-Introducing Christianity

An Eastern Apologia for a Western Audience

Amir Azarvan, editor

WIPF & STOCK · Eugene, Oregon

RE-INTRODUCING CHRISTIANITY
An Eastern Apologia for a Western Audience

Copyright © 2016 Wipf and Stock Publishers. All rights reserved. Except for brief quotations in critical publications or reviews, no part of this book may be reproduced in any manner without prior written permission from the publisher. Write: Permissions, Wipf and Stock Publishers, 199 W. 8th Ave., Suite 3, Eugene, OR 97401.

Wipf & Stock
An Imprint of Wipf and Stock Publishers
199 W. 8th Ave., Suite 3
Eugene, OR 97401

www.wipfandstock.com

PAPERBACK ISBN: 978-1-4982-2404-8
HARDCOVER ISBN: 978-1-4982-2406-2

Manufactured in the U.S.A.

There are so many people who have in various direct and indirect ways helped me in bringing this book to completion: My wife, whose love, patience, encouragement and sense of humor have sustained me over the years; My children, who are daily reminders of God's love for me; My inimitably selfless parents, without whose support this book could not have ever been published; My brother, for always inspiring me to do good, most recently through his new initiative, Just a Little Push (JustALittlePush.com), which engages in creative altruistic projects; Fr. Panayiotis Papageorgiou, for his spiritual guidance and assistance in reviewing contributions to this book; Last, but obviously not least, the twenty contributors of this volume, who have honored me by taking time out of their busy and productive lives to make this book a reality.

Contents

Contributors / xi

Part 1: Introduction

1 A Brief Introduction to Orthodoxy / *Amir Azarvan* / 3

Part 2: Basic Issues That Confront Most Christians

2 The Reality of God / *Fr. Jonathan Tobias* / 15

3 The Historical Jesus / *Eugenia Constantinou* / 24

4 The Resurrection of Jesus Christ / *Eugenia Constantinou* / 45

5 A Second Look at the God of the Old Testament / *Fr. Lawrence Farley* / 56

Part 3: The Church and Her Teaching

6 Bible Only? The Orthodox Teaching on Sola Scriptura / *Fr. John Whiteford* / 65

7 On Biblical Literalism / *Gayle Woloschak* / 77

8 Free from the Law? On the Rules of Orthodoxy and Their Purpose / *Mother Melania* / 81

CONTENTS

9   Respect for Women and the Tradition of the Male Priesthood / *Sister Margarete Roeber* / 87

10   Is Orthodoxy an Ethnically Exclusive Religion? / *Fr. Ernesto Obregon* / 92

Part 4: The Process of Salvation

11   The Problem of "Original Sin" / *Fr. Panayiotis Papageorgiou* / 99

12   Are We Saved by Faith Alone? The Orthodox View on the Doctrine of Sola Fide / *Fr. Steven Ritter* / 104

13   The Three-Fold Way / *Kyriacos C. Markides* / 109

14   Once Saved, Always Saved? / *Joshua Packwood* / 115

Part 5: Toward *Theosis*

15   Is Asceticism Just an "Eastern Thing"? / *James J. Miller* / 121

16   Why We Recite "Scripted" Prayers / *Fr. Michael Bressem* / 125

17   Are We Violating the Second Commandment? The Orthodox Teaching on Icons / *Robert Arakaki* / 132

18   Love in Action: The Orthodox Teaching on Almsgiving / *Fr. Kevin Gregory Long* / 137

19   The Orthodox View on Infant Baptism / *Fr. Josiah Trenham* / 142

20   The Eucharist Is Life / *Paraskevè (Eve) Tibbs* / 147

21   Why Must I Confess My Sins to a Priest? / *Mother Melania* / 155

Part 6: Our Friends in Christ

22   Why All the Focus on Mary? The Orthodox Teaching on the Theotokos / *Fr. Steven Ritter* / 163

23   The Communion of Saints / *David C. Ford* / 167

24   On the Importance of Spiritual Fathers / *Amir Azarvan* / 173

CONTENTS

Part 7: The Life to Come

25 Dwelling in the Love of God: Heaven and Hell as Our Response to God's Love / *Jonathan Resmini* / 183

Bibliography / 189

Contributors

Dr. Robert Arakaki administers the Orthodox-Reformed Bridge website (http://blogs.ancientfaith.com/orthodoxbridge), "a meeting place for Evangelicals, Reformed and orthodox Christians." He is also an adjunct professor at Hawaii Tokai International College.

Dr. Amir Azarvan is a political science professor at Georgia Gwinnett College in Lawrenceville, Georgia. His scholarly work has appeared in such venues as the *Journal of North African Studies* and the *Catholic Social Science Review*. He blogs (occasionally) at Amirica (WelcometoAmirica.blogspot.com).

Fr. (Dr.) Michael Bressem is the author of numerous articles on Orthodox theology, and is the co-owner of, and a provider at, a Christian ecumenical psychological services clinic in Hawaii. He serves as a deacon at Holy Theotokos of Iveron Russian Orthodox Church in Honolulu, Hawaii.

Dr. Eugenia Constantinou is an author and professor of Biblical Studies and Early Christianity at the University of San Diego, in San Diego, California, and the Franciscan School of Theology in Oceanside, California. She also hosts a popular podcast, *Search the Scriptures*, on Ancient Faith Radio.

Fr. Lawrence Farley is the pastor of St. Herman's Orthodox Church in Langley, British Columbia. He is also the author of the *Orthodox Bible Study Companion Series*.

CONTRIBUTORS

Dr. David Ford is an associate professor of church history at St. Tikhon's Orthodox Theological Academy in South Canaan, Pennsylvania. He has written two books, *Marriage as a Path to Holiness: Lives of Married Saints* (coauthored with his wife, Dr. Mary Ford), and *Women and Men in the Early Church: The Full Views of Saint John Chrysostom.*

Fr. Kevin Long is the pastor at St. Elias Orthodox Church in New Castle, Pennsylvania. For years, Fr. Kevin has been involved in pan-Orthodox initiatives and programs aimed at improving interfaith relations.

Dr. Kyriacos Markides is a sociology professor at the University of Maine in Orono, Maine. He has written several highly acclaimed books on Orthodox Christianity, including *The Mountain of Silence: A Search for Orthodox Spirituality.*

James Miller is an instructor at Southcentral Kentucky Community & Technical College, in Bowling Green, Kentucky. His research interests are in asceticism, vernacular religion, radical movements, and Orthodox theology.

Fr. Ernesto Obregon is currently attached to the Greek Orthodox Cathedral in Birmingham, Alabama, and is an adjunct professor of world religions at the Florida Institute of Technology in Melbourne, Florida.

Dr. Joshua Packwood is an assistant professor of philosophy at the University of Arkansas in Fort Smith, Arkansas. He is also a Senior Fellow at the Sophia Institute, and the author of a forthcoming textbook entitled, *Introduction to Philosophy: A Global Approach.*

Fr. (Dr.) Panayiotis Papageorgiou is the pastor of Holy Transfiguration Greek Orthodox Church in Marietta, Georgia. He holds a PhD in theology from the Catholic University of America.

Jonathan Resmini is a graduate of Holy Cross Greek Orthodox School of Theology in Brookline, Massachusetts, and is pursuing a PhD at the Boston University School of Theology. His research interests include Orthodox spirituality, ecclesiology, and the phenomenological and empirical study of religious and spiritual practices and experiences.

Contributors

Fr. Steven Ritter is the pastor at St. James Antiochian Orthodox Mission in Buford, Georgia, and hosts *The Life of the Church Today*, a podcast on Ancient Faith Radio. He is the author of *That Your Joy May Be Full—Learning from the Authentic Orthodox Theology of the Spirit*.

Sister Margarete (Roeber) is a rassaphore nun at Holy Assumption Monastery in Calistoga, CA. She also holds an MA in applied theology from Balamand University, through the Antiochian Orthodox Archdiocese of North America.

Mother Melania (Salem) is the superior of Holy Assumption Monastery in Calistoga, California, and the author of numerous children's books. She holds a PhD in theology from the University of Durham.

Dr. Eve Tibbs is an affiliate associate professor of theology at Fuller Theological Seminary in Pasadena, California, and has served as chair of the Eastern Orthodox Studies Group of the American Academy of Religion.

Fr. Jonathan Tobias is a professor of pastoral theology at Christ the Saviour Seminary in Johnstown, Pennsylvania, as well as a priest in the American Carpatho-Russian Diocese.

Fr. (Dr.) Josiah Trenham is an adjunct professor at St. Katherine College in Encinitas, California, and the pastor at St. Andrew Orthodox Church in Riverside. He is also the founder and director of *Patristic Nectar Publications*.

Fr. John Whiteford is the pastor at St. Jonah Orthodox Church in Spring, Texas. His weekly homilies and lectures are available online via *From the Amvon*, a podcast on Ancient Faith Radio.

Dr. Gayle Woloschak is the president of the Orthodox Theological Society of America, as well as a radiology professor at the Northwestern University Feinberg School of Medicine in Chicago, Illinois.

PART 1

Introduction

1

A Brief Introduction to Orthodoxy

Amir Azarvan

Man was born for joy, not for sorrow.
—Elder Avvakum the Barefoot

WHEN ST. PAUL INTRODUCED Christianity to the Athenians, he did so by promoting his faith in ways that were familiar to, and respectful of, his audience (Acts 17: 22–23). He did not speak of God as a wholly foreign deity, but as the hitherto Unknown God whom they were already worshipping. In more recent times—toward the end of the eighteenth century—the Russian missionaries who preached to Alaska's native population presented Christianity "not as the abolition, but as the fulfillment, of the Aleut's ancient religious heritage."[1] These are but two examples of an ongoing tradition of situating Christianity within the specific context of an audience, partly in order to make the seemingly unfamiliar familiar to it.

Of the various ways that I, personally, could familiarize the reader of this particular work with Orthodox Christianity, I have chosen not to stress continuities between religious traditions, but to present Orthodoxy in light of modern society's struggle to satisfy the universal desire for lasting happiness.[2] Researchers from the World Health Organization tell us that people in

---

1. Stokoe and Oleksa, *Orthodox Christians in North America (1794–1994)*.

2. This universal desire is twofold. First, we all desire happiness. This is true even of the suicidal, for they do not seek to take their own lives because they wish to be unhappy, but simply because they tragically believe that happiness is unattainable. Second, we also want our happiness to be everlasting. No one tires of being happy, although they might wish to replace the source of their happiness with another from time to time.

PART 1—INTRODUCTION

wealthier countries are more prone to depression than those in low-income countries.[3] In the United States, as in other Western countries, depression has risen steadily over the past several decades.[4] While the causes of depression are obviously multifaceted, the decline in religiosity has arguably contributed to this trend. After all, the preponderance of empirical evidence indicates that "levels of happiness are greatest amongst religious folks."[5]

Without wishing to reduce Orthodoxy to a quick, feel-good philosophy,[6] I believe that a case can be made that it is especially well-suited to contribute to the fulfillment of this universal desire.[7] In the following five sections, I introduce the reader to some of the more salient aspects of Orthodoxy, relating each of them to this particular theme. After briefly discussing the goal of this volume, I then lay out each of its chapters, which delve much more deeply into these aspects.

An Experiential Faith

Before I met my wife, I had a reasonable, but wavering faith that I would one day find "the one"—someone with whom I would wish to spend the rest of my life. Now that I have found her, I no longer doubt her existence, since I *experience* the reality of her existence on a daily basis.

This is analogous to the Orthodox approach to God. Today, faith in God's existence appears to rest largely on philosophical reasoning. Accordingly, Christian apologists advance various logical arguments for God's existence, some more persuasive than others. Of course, appeals to reason are not, in and of themselves, bad.[8] But when faith is loosened from its spiritual mooring, it becomes "a mere and easily replaceable theory, rather than a living reality."[9] The purpose of Orthodox spirituality is to transform

---

3. MacMillan, "People in Affluent Nations."
4. Matilda, "Rate of Depression on the Rise."
5. Routledge, "Are Religious People Happier?"
6. The novice would be wise to recall the words of St. Syncletica: "All must endure great travail and conflict when they are first converted to the Lord, but later they have unspeakable joy." Ward, *Desert Fathers*, 15.
7. I have discovered in my own survey research of Orthodox Christians that those who are more spiritually involved report significantly higher levels of happiness.
8. Indeed, Fr. Jonathan Tobias makes use of scientific reasoning in grounding his claim for God's existence (see ch. 2).
9. Azarvan, "Are Highly Theistic Countries Dumber?," 157.

the believer in such a way that his or her beliefs no longer rest "on the shaky ground of rational speculation," but are established "on the solid basis of mystical [i.e., experiential] validation."[10] This process, which Kyriacos Markides refers to as the three hold way, begins with *catharsis*, or the purification of the soul from all self-centered desires. It is through this process, and not through philosophical reasoning, that we acquire knowledge of God's existence. This is perhaps why, in my survey research on Orthodox Christians, I discovered that spiritual involvement[11] was significantly associated with greater faith in God's existence.

In short, true faith is not synonymous with a blind hope or a reasonable guess, but with experiential knowledge. I have long been fond of quoting the following words from a contemporary elder of the church:

> Those who wish to investigate whether God exists must employ the appropriate methodology which is none other than the purification of the heart from egotistical passions and impurities. If people manage to cleanse their hearts and still fail to see God, then they are justified by concluding that indeed God is a lie.[12]

A Sacramental Faith

While many modern strains of Christianity have, in a sense, forced God from the sacraments (literally "mysteries"), reducing them to mere symbols, the Orthodox continue to view them as channels of grace, mystically uniting believers with God. As Fr. Thomas Fitzgerald explains, the Holy Mysteries are not limited to the seven sacraments of baptism, chrismation,[13] the eucharist (or communion), confession, ordination, marriage, and unction (or healing): "*All* our life and the creation of which we are an important part points to and reveals God" (emphasis added).[14]

This sacramental worldview is not unrelated to this chapter's focus on happiness, as empirical research on differences between Roman

---

10. Ibid.

11. I measured this variable in terms of the frequency with which one attends church, prays, fasts according to the prescribed fasting days of the church, keeps vigil, reads spiritual works, and participates in the sacraments of confession and holy communion.

12. Markides, *Mountain of Silence*, 44.

13. This is the sacrament that immediately follows baptism, whereby the believer is given the gift of the Holy Spirit through anointing with holy oil.

14. Fitzgerald, *Sacraments*.

PART 1—INTRODUCTION

Catholics—who similarly practice a deeply sacramental faith, and are more extensively studied than the Orthodox—and Protestants suggests.[15] Benno Torlinger and Christophe Schaltegger partially attribute Catholics' reportedly lower suicide rate to their communitarian ethos, which provides a higher level of social support to the believer:

> Whereas the Catholic view of the world as God's sacrament and a natural good for humans encourages a social response to God, the Protestant view of human society as God-forsaken, unnatural, and oppressive promotes a view of the individual standing against society rather than being integrated into it.[16]

In addition, Franz Höllinger and colleagues suggest that its greater stress on rituals and symbols makes Catholicism "more attractive for the masses, and thus leads to higher levels of religious participation and of religious beliefs."[17] By recalling the religiosity-happiness link noted above, we may conclude that, through its mediating effects on religious faith and practice, sacramental Christianity is an effective safeguard of happiness.[18]

An Ascetical Faith

To go against self is the beginning of salvation.

—Evagrius the Solitary

This is the ultimate law—the seed dies to live, the bread must be cast upon the waters, he that loses his soul will save it.

—C. S. Lewis

---

15. My intention here is not to attack a particular branch of Christianity or treat Protestants as a monolith, but to simply build a case for sacramentalism.

16. Torgler and Schaltegger, "New Evidence on Differences," 316–40. See also Becker and Woessmann, "Knocking on Heaven's Door?"

17. Höllinger et al., "Christian Religion, Society," 133–57.

18. Using the latest US data from the World Values Survey, I discovered that Catholics were significantly more likely to report personal happiness than Protestants, even after adjusting for age, income, and sex. To access data, visit http://www.worldvaluessurvey.org.

"The thing you long for," wrote C. S. Lewis, "summons you away from the self."[19] The Orthodox way consists of ascetical disciplines that are designed to bring about this transcendence of self. St. Theophan the Recluse succinctly summarizes these disciplines:

> These, then, are the activities and exercised which are the means of healing our powers and bringing them back to our lost purity and wholeness: fasting, labor, vigil, solitude, withdrawal from the world, control of the senses, reading of the scriptures and the Holy Fathers, attendance at church, frequent confession and communion.[20]

Here the reader might be struck by an apparent paradox. How could self-denial possibly enhance one's joy, which I argue is the end result of participating in the Orthodox spiritual life? Is it not more correct to suggest that Christianity is a religion of killjoys who abstain from every pleasure?

It is true that if pleasure is defined synonymously with *hedonism*—or the pursuit of material pleasure—then Orthodoxy is unequivocally pleasure-denying (and this is how the term "pleasure" is normally employed in patristic writings). But pleasure is also synonymous with *happiness*. With this latter meaning in mind, one might reasonably suggest that ascetically-minded people are not only true pleasure seekers, but are also more successful in their pursuit. For, while modern society has long assumed that happiness rests on the acquisition of material goods, scientific evidence has consistently shown that materialists are significantly *less* happy.[21]

A Legalistic Faith?

Many skeptics, as well as many contemporary believers, will fault Orthodoxy for being too "legalistic." The church does, to be sure, prescribe rules, such as when and from what to fast. When we lose sight of the purpose for which these rules were designed—spiritual healing and everlasting joy—they appear to us as unnecessary or even oppressive. But the truth is that the church is no more "legalistic"—with all of the negative connotations that the term carries—than the doctor who prescribes medicine for the bodily healing of his patient. Also, consider the words of St. Thalassios:

---

19. Lewis, *Problem of Pain*, 154.
20. Theophan the Recluse, "Fruits of Prayer," 139.
21. Tsang et al., "Why Are Materialists Less Happy?," 62–66.

PART 1—INTRODUCTION

"You will not find the rigors of the ascetic life hard to bear if you do all things with measure and by rule."[22] Here, rules are said to facilitate ascetical work, which as was suggested above, ultimately fosters true happiness.

A Communal Faith

No one can attain to God unless he first passes through his fellow men.

—St. Porphyrios of Kafsokalivia

"We are condemned alone, but are only saved with others." Variations of this aphorism express the Orthodox understanding that Christianity is not a "me and Jesus only" religion.[23] As Metropolitan Kallistos Ware explains, "God is salvation, and God's saving power is mediated to humans in His Body, the Church."[24] Hence why we ask, in addition to God, fellow believers—both living and departed—for their support. Just like how we "pray" (in the King James Bible sense of the term) to friends and family for their intercession, the Orthodox also pray to the saints on the assumption that the prayers of righteous people do, indeed, avail much (cf. Jas 5:16).[25]

This understanding of salvation is also reflected in our corporate worship—that is, our participation in the divine liturgy (the Greek term *leitourgia*, from which "liturgy" derives, is directly translated as "*common work*"). Regrettably, many have come to question the importance of attending church. I recall asking a neighbor one Sunday whether she had gone to church that morning (not because I am the religious police, but simply because I could not think of anything else to talk about at the time). Attesting to the atomization of Christian worship—if, indeed, we can call it that—she replied: "Nah, we decided to stay at home and watch the sermon

---

22. Thalassios, "On Love, Self-Control and Life," 319.

23. We find this communal ethos reflected in the Lord's Prayer (Matt 6:9–13), where *our* Father, and not *my* Father, is invoked.

24. This is not to say those are visibly outside of the church are necessarily damned. As Ware points out, "There may be members of the Church who are not visibly such, but whose membership is known to God alone." Ware, *Orthodox Church*, 247–48.

25. In its earlier usage, the term "prayer" was not restricted in meaning to worship, which of is course due to God, alone. There are numerous examples of this broader usage in the King James Version of the Bible. For instance, Bathsheba was not worshipping King Solomon when she entreated, "I pray thee, say me not nay" (1 Kgs 2:20).

online." Presenting a starkly different view of the importance of collective worship—not in cyberspace, but in an actual, physical location—Christos Yannaras views the liturgy of the church not simply as

> an expression of religious worship, but [as] the core and sum of her life and truth, of her faith and ethics. The life and truth of the Church, her faith and her ethos are a *liturgy*, an organic function of a unified body which receives man in order to save him. (emphasis in original)[26]

Not only is there a soteriological reason for worshipping together as one body, but there is a psychological one, as well. Returning, once again, to the theme of this chapter, it has been demonstrated that church attendance has a significantly positive impact on reported happiness,[27] and it is not difficult to understand why. Religious attendees enjoy higher levels of social support, and "higher levels of social support lead to higher levels of psychological well-being."[28] Furthermore, it appears that the specifically religious character of this form of social interaction is not merely incidental to these benefits. As Lim explains, "Friendship in church is more strongly correlated with life satisfaction than friendships in other contexts such as the workplace or a book club."[29]

The Goal of This Volume

Today, many apologetical works seem to be written in a condescending, self-righteous manner; the subtext being, "Here's why being X [whatever religion you please] makes us better than you!" Instead, our goal is to communicate in an honest, yet non-adversarial way, the following message to the reader: "Here is why we invite you to explore the faith that has brought us so much hope and joy." To those readers who believe that we have to some extent failed in this effort, I offer my sincere apologies.

---

26. Yannaras, *Freedom of Morality*, 85.
27. Cohen-Zada and Sander, "Religious Participation versus Shopping," 889–906.
28. Routledge, "Are Religious People Happier."
29. Lim, "In U.S., Churchgoers Boast Better Mood."

Part 1—Introduction

Chapters

The following brief chapters build upon and go beyond the aspects of Orthodox Christianity introduced above. Part 2 of this book addresses challenges to the Christian faith that should be familiar to most believers—not just the Orthodox. Fr. Jonathan Tobias (ch. 2) explores the roles that science, philosophy, culture, and spirituality play in revealing to us the reality of God. Jeannie Constantinou (ch. 3) evaluates popular theories that purport to debunk the Church's traditional understanding of who the Jesus of history actually was. She then (ch. 4) explains the historicity of the defining event of Christianity: the resurrection of Christ. Fr. Lawrence Farley (ch. 5) provides the lens through which the Orthodox view the God of the Old Testament.

Part 3 deals with fundamental points on which Orthodoxy and other Christian faiths diverge. Fr. John Whiteford (ch. 6) critically examines the doctrine of *sola scriptura*, the teaching that that the Scriptures, alone, are authoritative for the faith and practice of the believer. Gayle Woloschak (ch. 7) expresses the Orthodox view on divine inspiration, and discusses Orthodoxy's historic rejection of biblical literalism. While Orthodoxy might give the impression that it is a rule-centered faith, Mother Melania (ch. 8) explains that rules are valued not for their own sake, but as a means to the fundamental end of Orthodox spirituality: union with God. Sister Margarete Roeber (ch. 9) tackles a highly sensitive subject—the exclusively male priesthood of traditional Christianity—and relates her discussion to Orthodoxy's (possibly surprising) view of woman. Fr. Ernesto Obregon (ch. 10) provides the historical context in which to properly understand the strongly ethnic character of many Orthodox parishes, while stressing the universal mission of the church.

Part 4 builds on the previous section by introducing Orthodoxy's teachings on salvation, which remain largely unfamiliar to Christians (and their detractors) in the West. Fr. Panayiotis Papageorgiou (ch. 11) discusses the Augustinian view of original sin, which has shaped much of modern Christianity's theological development, and distinguishes it from the Orthodox teaching on ancestral sin. Fr. Steven Ritter (ch. 12) discusses the doctrine of *sola fide*—another teaching that is at odds with the Orthodox tradition—which holds that faith, alone, is what secures one's salvation. Kyriacos Markides (ch. 13) expounds on Orthodoxy's understanding of salvation as a process—as opposed to a singular event—that unfolds through the stages of purification, illumination, and deification. Joshua Packwood (ch. 14) addresses the contentious question of whether salvation can be lost.

Part 5 introduces the content and purpose of Orthodox asceticism. James Miller (ch. 15) discusses the integral role that asceticism has always played in Orthodox spirituality. Fr. Michael Bressem (ch. 16) explains why the Orthodox recite composed (or "scripted") prayers, in addition to the spontaneous (or "free style") prayers, which are far more common among Western Christians. Robert Arakaki (ch. 17) provides the historical and scriptural bases for the use of icons in prayer. Whereas many skeptics view Christians as, at best, apathetic about the poor—regrettably, this is increasingly true of many self-professing believers—Fr. Kevin Long (ch. 18) emphasizes almsgiving as a necessary ascetical labor (as St. Cyprian noted, alms "deliver from death, and . . . purges away sins").

The next three chapters concern the Holy Mysteries—i.e., the sacraments—of the Orthodox faith. Reasoning from both Scripture and historical practice, Fr. Josiah Trenham (ch. 19) explains why children in the Orthodox Church are baptized before they have acquired the ability to reason. Eve Tibbs (ch. 20) presents the Orthodox understanding of holy communion, the "sacraments of sacraments," which forms the center of Orthodox worship. Mother Melania (ch. 21) addresses concerns regarding the mystery of confession—a sacrament that appears increasingly out of place where ego-centered spirituality and legalistic conceptions of sin hold sway.

Part 6 concerns the saints and elders of the church, whose lives and counsel humble, guide, and instill hope in the believer. Fr. Steven (ch. 22) explains the importance that the Orthodox—and, indeed, all Christians until relatively recent times—have assigned to the Virgin Mary. David Ford (ch. 23) broadens the focus to discuss the integral role that saints, in general, play in our spiritual lives. I (ch. 24) draw from both Scripture and analogical reasoning in laying the Orthodox rationale for embarking on the spiritual path under the careful guidance of an elder.

Part 7 deals with questions concerning the afterlife. What exactly are heaven and hell? Is the latter a literal lake of fire created by God to torment all non-self-professing Christians? Jonathan Resmini (ch. 25) closes this book by offering Orthodox responses to these sensitive questions.

PART 2

Basic Issues That Confront Most Christians

2

The Reality of God

Fr. Jonathan Tobias

Is GOD REAL? A better question, from an Orthodox perspective, is "How is it possible *not* to believe, or know, that God is real?" Christian Orthodoxy has always claimed that all of reality points to God. Every "thing" is understood as a sign of God's presence. Orthodoxy has said, too, that everyone is born with the ability to notice this divine significance of creation in every single moment of consciousness.

But is this comprehensive interpretation of phenomena just a prejudice, merely the fruit of religious conviction? There is certainly a lot of disagreement with this view of reality, and much of it is honest, thoughtful and well-intended. There are many people—educated and less-educated alike—who believe that science disagrees that "natural" reality has anything to do with God. They believe strongly that science has proven that religion is false, and that there is no God. Some popular intellectuals say as much. Writers and speakers like Richard Dawkins forcefully claim that there is nothing beyond physical reality, and that it is only through scientific observation that things can be known.

Is There Anything beyond Physical Reality?

The difficulty with this precept is that "physical reality" is something that is never directly perceived. Materialistic philosophy holds that observation is necessary for reality to be known, or "believed in." The difficulty is that observation is never direct—at least for humans. The five "senses" of touch, sight, hearing, smell and taste (and there may be more) are all the products of photo-electrical or piezo-electrical stimulation. The stimulation starts with nerve endings in an organ of the body (like the eye or the skin) and ends up processed and interpreted by various parts of the physical brain.

What is important, here, is that the presentation of the sensory information is not directly received, but is experienced in the consciousness—and this experience is very different from the original data from the nerve endings. Nothing is "observed" without this perception first having gone through the processing of the consciousness. This is true even of insights gained from strictly-controlled experiments performed in the hard sciences.

Why is this important? The human consciousness is the awareness of its own existence in the here-and-now. It is the constant thought, the experiencing and the decision-making that is always going on in the human mind, especially in the waking moments. It is impossible to think about or study anything outside of the consciousness. Instead of assuming that consciousness is "contained" by material reality, or that it is just a product of processes, it is just as conceivable to think that physical reality is contained by consciousness. Indeed, scientists are showing appreciation for the growing body of evidence pointing to "the survival of consciousness, following bodily death," as well as "the existence of other levels of reality that are non-physical."[1] And this is exactly what theistic religion has always suggested. There is an "infinite consciousness" that causes and contains all material reality. Consciousness, therefore, is not located in the brain.

There are some scientific guesses about what the consciousness is and how it operates: none of these guesses have been confirmed by the scientific process. One of the better of these guesses is suggested by atheist philosopher J. J. C. Smart, who contends that the consciousness is actually a "proprioception," in which one part of the brain supervises (or watches over) the activity of other parts of the brain.[2] Another is that the consciousness is the result of quantum activity. This suggestion is known as the famous Penrose-Hameroff theory, which proposes that consciousness arises from quantum interchanges within microtubules within the brain.[3]

These guesses are legitimate scientific hypotheses. But there is another hypothesis that is not so legitimate: that consciousness does not exist at all,

---

1. Beauregard et al., "Manifesto for a Post-Materialist Science."
2. Cited in Hart, *Experience of God*, 205.
3. Penrose, *Emperor's New Mind*.

or that it is only "background noise" from all the electrical activity in the brain, or that which is called "consciousness" is only an illusion.

Even though the first two guesses are legitimate hypotheses, there remains no scientific evidence for these guesses. And the third, illegitimate guess has been a powerful idea for the past several centuries. The idea is that if a phenomenon (like consciousness) cannot be explicable in a physical, material sense, then it must not exist. This idea is the central proposition of a trend that has been given various labels, like "naturalism" or "scientism." In this discussion, I use the term "materialism."

Materialism is a philosophic—not scientific—doctrine that followed the development of modern science, but did not *result* from it. It complicates the discussion about the reality of God. God—as God—is completely beyond physicality, as he would logically have to be for physicality to exist at all. But if one's ideas about reality are completely biased against a nonphysical reality, then however could the reality of God be considered fairly? Science seeks to observe nature and tries to discover the laws by which nature operates. It refuses to say anything about what it cannot observe and quantify.

Science Pointing to God's Reality

Science actually reports a great deal of evidence pointing to the reality of God. One does not have to be religious at all to notice this. The scientific and mathematical view of the world that was framed by Isaac Newton showed a universe that was lawful, and therefore predictable. It was also even more beautiful, and much larger and more complex than had been thought before.

However, these Newtonian laws gave the impression that the universe was infinite in size, and infinite in time (both past and future). This is not the case. In the last century, the Newtonian view of reality was expanded in every way. Contrary to the idea that the universe is eternal, it is now known that the universe is 13.7 billion years old. Einstein stubbornly defended the idea that the universe had an "infinite past" until Hubble's observations so strongly indicated a "big bang."[4] That same number also represents the size of the universe: a radius of 13.7 billion light years from the central origin point of the big bang.

---

4. Douglas, "Forty Minutes with Einstein," 100.

Part 2—Basic Issues That Confront Most Christians

The old modernistic view of the universe has also been complicated by the unavoidable discovery of quantum mechanics (it is "unavoidable" because the search for solutions to problems in the Newtonian view led scientists inexorably into quantum mechanics). It is now known that that there are no "basic building blocks" of reality: the perception of reality does not stop at the atom with its protons, neutrons and electrons. Not only is there a host of new subatomic particles that constitute atoms, but the idea of "particles" themselves has changed. Instead of being "packets of material," subatomic particles are scientifically observed to be instantiations of energy interacting with various fields. This idea of "particles as energy" should be reminiscent of Einstein's famous formula $E = MC^2$. This formula is really about the complete interchangeability of matter and energy.

Further, a series of physical "constants" have been discovered and confirmed. These constants were not known prior to the last century. One of these constants is familiar: it is the speed of light (300,000 km/sec in a vacuum). Other constants relate to the smallest possible intervals of space and time, the four fundamental forces (i.e., gravity, electromagnetism, strong and weak nuclear forces), the rest mass of protons, neutrons and electrons, and the total rest mass of the universe (which is now thought to be 10^{53} kg).

The interesting, if not shocking, thing about these constants (and there are many of them), is that they could not be anything other than what they are—not even by an insignificant variance. The discovery of the fact that the universe has an undeniable beginning in time and space has produced questions with which science has to grapple. Conditions that were amenable to a stable physical existence and even life were established almost immediately after the moment of the big bang. Nothing can be taken for granted anymore, since there was such a beginning, and no phenomenon can be dismissed as "the way it always was"—because it was not. Why are there only four observable dimensions, and not more? Why is the proton so stable that its half-life is the age of the universe (vs. the half-life of a neutron, which is only ten minutes)? Why is the strong nuclear force about one hundred times stronger than the electromagnetic force? Because if that ratio were more or less, the material universe would either crush itself and never expand, or every atom would fly apart into an ever-expanding nebula of solitary subatomic particles.[5]

Some scientists would like to say that this exceedingly "life-friendly" set of conditions simply emerged by sheer chance. But others point out that the

5. Barr, *Modern Physics and Ancient Faith*, 118–37.

probability of these constants converging "on their own" is almost infinitely small. In fact, Roger Penrose, a renowned English mathematical physicist, calculates this probability as 1 in 10 raised to the power of 10, the exponent of which is itself raised to the power of 123.[6] This is an unbelievably large number. Robert J. Spitzer noted that if one were to write it as an ordinary number, the number itself would fill up a large portion of the universe.[7]

A few observations should be drawn here. First, the "Penrose number" just discussed is an infinitesimal probability. It is frequently suggested that the physical constants of the universe can be generated by chance, given enough iterations of the "big bang" (that is, if there really have been and will be an infinite series of iterations). The concept of "chance" is thus used in such a way that it embraces, in a single category, probabilities that are reasonable and those that are almost infinitely impossible events. There is real doubt as to whether there can be such an infinite series of iterations, given the fact that entropy makes such a series impossible. Moreover, there is substantial doubt as to whether there ever has been, or will be, any "big crunch" (or reversal of the single "big bang") at all. In 1989, it was discovered that the expansion of the universe actually started to speed up a few billion years ago.[8]

In addition, we have learned from Einstein and quantum mechanics that matter ultimately is not just "matter." Instead, the further and more profound the scientific investigation into the substance of the universe, the more clearly we see that what appears to us in our consciousness as "matter" is really a vastly complex interaction of energy with fields. Werner Heisenberg, an early pioneer in the study of quantum physics, noted that "the smallest units of matter are, in fact, not physical objects in the ordinary sense of the word: they are forms, structures, or—in Plato's sense—Ideas, which can be unambiguously spoken of only in the language of mathematics."[9]

Another observation is from quantum mechanics. And this is the strange truth that the very act of scientific measurement affects the placement or momentum of subatomic phenomena. It is clear that the old idea from Descartes that there is a clear division between the observer and the observed is no longer valid—at least at the subatomic level.

6. Penrose, *Emperor's New Mind*, 343.
7. Spitzer, *New Proofs for the Existence of God*, 58.
8. Ibid., 17.
9. Cited in Moevs, *Metaphysics of Dante's Comedy*, 188.

Yet another observation is that a natural law comes from higher, more complex laws that are less obvious, but more beautiful. No "order" or "organization" of things is ever produced by disordered or less organized systems. Simplicity never produces complexity by itself, but only under the operation of a higher, more complex law. The deeper one travels into the profound levels of the substance of the universe, the more one is astounded—even overcome—by a beauty that can only be articulated by higher math and a physics that is at once quantum and astrophysical.[10]

These observations point to the increasing weakness of the materialistic view. More than a few physicists and mathematicians are convinced that science demands a consideration of the reality of God; and not only that he is real, but that he is as all humans are able to know him: infinitely present in time and space, and absolute in being.

Some physicists believe that science will be able to go no further than to observe, at the deepest observations possible, that there exists a "supersymmetry," which itself may be the direct manifestation of transcendent design—something that Christian Orthodoxy would recognize as divine law. That is what philosophers like to call "natural knowledge." In other words, one needs no "unnatural assistance" to know these things. But the Orthodox Church says that this "natural knowledge" is still the result of "supernatural revelation": even after the observation of physical phenomena via the "scientific method," the inferences drawn will be the result of human work and active divine revelation.[11]

The Cross-Cultural Consensus on God's Reality

For thousands of years, humans have known this about God. They have been able to infer this from common human experience, and from disciplined observation. Other religions, not just Christianity, have talked about God in the same way—that he is infinitely conscious and all-knowing, that he is the transcendent source and constant cause of all being. The different

---

10. Barr, *Modern Physics and Ancient Faith*.

11. In a curious inversion of expectations, the sciences may turn out to be more open to the reality of God than the humanities. Even something as religious-sounding as "God's goodness" could be inferred from the strange incidence of the physical constants of the universe alone. Here modern physics shows more than a little similarity to the early cosmology of Aristotle and Ptolemy, which asserted that as one's perception ascended higher from the earth, the more reality became beautiful and unbroken.

religions and cultural traditions agree on these truths with remarkably similar propositions.[12]

This universal, cross-cultural consensus about God should not be interpreted as some "primitive stage" in human social evolution—where religion, or belief in God, is some lesser state. This interpretation wrongly assumes that modern civilization must be better than older civilizations. In particular, the assumption is that societies must become better as they become more technologically developed.

History says otherwise. The last century was more technologically advanced than any before it. It was also more "secularized" in that belief in God was the most displaced by materialism. Nevertheless, the twentieth century was the bloodiest by far. A case can be made that the twentieth century was also the most barbaric.

Despite the materialistic dominance of contemporary society, the fact remains that humans can still perceive God as ultimate being, as infinite consciousness—even in, and especially in, their own consciousness, and in the experience of everyday life. This should not be surprising, since every single "thing" in creation reveals itself as entirely analogous to—even if infinitely separate from—the Creator. Outside of the "Cartesian" view of reality, the "observer" and the "observed" are one and the same. It was Descartes, after all, who wedged an "interruption" between the two, in which he said it was possible to "know about" something objectively, without knowing that something in relationship (or in "communion"). This Cartesian division of the subject from the object was a new thing, but because of the clear effect of observation upon quantum phenomena, it may be scientifically obsolete.

Reflections on Suffering

If there is anything that blinds some to the reality of God, it is the hardship of human history. "If God is good and all-powerful, why do bad things happen in the world?" This question Christian Orthodoxy tries to answer by pointing to the chaos produced by the evil, resulting, in turn, from the abuse of our free will. But the harder questions are these: Why did evil happen in this particular event? Why did suffering happen to me, or to a loved one? Why this particular form of suffering, which did *not* follow from my choices? Orthodoxy responds with frustrating simplicity: These are the

---

12. It would be difficult to overestimate the value of David Bentley Hart to this particular discussion. See Hart, *Experience of God*.

questions against which all strictly natural arguments for the existence of God fail.

As I explain in the following section, what is needed is what faith—that is, the experience of Christian Orthodoxy—provides. Faith enables the sufferer to enter into solidarity with the Person of Christ. Christ as Infinite God entered into history as a particular human, and experienced—exhaustively—all the violence and injustice of history. In doing so, he, the "prover" of God's reality as infinite beauty and absolute peace, cancelled the permanence of violence in human nature, and established a resolution of all suffering—but in the age to come, when space-time is integrated with eternity. Of course, that age is practiced, perceived and somewhat experienced even now. But it is an incomplete experience as yet.

Beyond Dialectical Reasoning: Faith and Knowledge of God's Reality

There is a knowledge that goes beyond natural knowledge. It is a knowledge of things that really cannot be observed scientifically. It is a knowledge that apprehends realities that are beyond the boundaries of space and time. It is the knowledge that each creature in creation has not only a meaning, but also a destiny. It is the knowledge that every human can perceive material and immaterial realities; that a human can not only know about God, but to know God himself in communion.

This knowledge that is "above" nature is called "faith." As St. Paul once said, this faith is "the substance of things hoped for, the evidence of things not seen" (Heb 11:1). The phrases "things hoped for" and "things not seen" refer to the realm of knowledge that is beyond space-time. Here, faith obviously does not refer to an emotional condition of "confidence." It denotes instead a certain knowledge of reality.

The highest point of faith knows God not only as divine nature (which is the limit of natural knowledge), but that God is a oneness of three persons. Knowing God as Trinity is the highest knowledge, and is utterly beyond science and natural knowledge.[13] This knowledge that is called "faith"

---

13. Faith is actually analogous to the lower science of natural knowledge. Just as any science will adapt itself to the object of its investigation, so also faith moves the believer to act according to the form of faith. And another word for this "form" of faith is "Orthodox religion"—with all its sacraments, ascetical traditions of prayer and fasting, liturgy, and adherence to holy tradition. As Hart explains, "[Any] search, if it is to be successful,

is produced by solidarity with Jesus Christ and participation in his body, the church. It is an experiential knowledge that results from a free participation in the life of Christ, and communion with the Holy Trinity.

This "supra-rational" knowledge of a reality beyond space-time—this "faith"—cannot be confined to rational knowledge, but it continues to involve it. The Orthodox faith carries along rationality and logic into the higher realms of "theology," where the Trinity is most clearly experienced and known.[14] Natural knowledge can only offer abstract rational thoughts about God, but Orthodox theology that is experienced in doctrinal thought, participation in the sacraments, and hard work in prayer, fasting and almsgiving is faith that actually knows God directly. In faith, the God that everyone already knows "about" (or should) is *experienced* through Jesus Christ, the Word.

From the vantage point of this faith, one turns back and perceives that there is One Who was revealing, to every human mind, the God Who made all things, Who is the First and Efficient Cause of all things, Who is the Perfecter of all things in the Last Day when space-time will be integrated with eternity. That One is the Revealer of God to the world: and it is only fitting, then, that Jesus Christ, the Second Person of the Trinity, is called "God the Word."

When the Orthodox Church calls Jesus Christ the "word" (or *Logos*), the church is recognizing the truth that, ultimately, he is the greatest (and really, the *only*) "prover" of the reality of God to the human mind.

---

must be conducted in a manner fitted to the reality one is looking for." Hart, *Experience of God*, 320.

14. Fr. John Romanides emphasizes that faith—as opposed to rational, natural knowledge—is an "empirical science," in which knowledge is gained through experience, leading up to the ultimate "vision," or *"theoria,"* of the Holy Trinity. This vision is not of God in his essence, but in his energies (i.e., his "presence"). See the best summation of his teachings in Vlachos, *Empirical Dogmatics of the Orthodox Catholic Church*.

3

The Historical Jesus

Eugenia Constantinou

WHO WAS THE HISTORICAL Jesus? A harmless hippie? A revolutionary zealot? False prophet? Gentle teacher? Misguided messiah? Wise philosopher? A charismatic rabbi whose fanatical followers catapulted him from a merely human messiah to "the Lord"? Debate has swirled around the identity and life of Jesus since the moment he began his public ministry.

The Historical Jesus

As a historical person, Jesus was an itinerant first-century rabbi (a Hebrew word which means "teacher"). Born in Bethlehem but raised in the village of Nazareth in the northern region of Galilee, he began a ministry of teaching and healing when he was about thirty years old. He was a charismatic preacher and phenomenal wonderworker and rapidly acquired many followers ("disciples") who numbered in the thousands. His ministry was unconventional. His words and his actions were shocking, even outrageous, for any Jew but especially for a rabbi. His ministry was inclusive, not exclusive. He welcomed to his movement all sorts of people, both within mainstream Judaism and those shunned by it, pious and influential Jews, as well as the poor, uneducated, former tax collectors and repentant prostitutes and sinners. He taught that all were welcome into the kingdom of heaven: God loves everyone, and will forgive anything, if one only repents and forgives others.

Although thousands followed him as disciples, he chose only twelve men to form an inner circle of leadership. Eventually the Twelve would become the most important leaders of the early Christian church. Jesus' followers were convinced that Jesus was the Messiah, a long-awaited leader whom many Jews expected would deliver them from Roman occupation and restore an independent kingdom of Israel. His followers believed Jesus was the Messiah because he fulfilled Jewish prophecies written hundred years before his birth. Perhaps the most publically prominent displays of this prophetic fulfillment were his extraordinary and abundant miracles (Isa 35:4–6). No one had ever performed such wonders before and no one has since.

Jesus encouraged people to pursue inner purity (of heart, soul and mind) not merely an outer, legalistic "ritual" purity followed by all Jews at that time, called the "law of Moses." The law of Moses is not the same as the Ten Commandments. Rather, it is a complex system of thousands of rules that regulate daily Jewish life and set standards for whether one is "righteous" (acceptable to God) or not. "Ritual purity" includes ritual washings before or after certain activities, avoiding touching ritually "unclean" objects, not associating with ritually "unclean" people, eating only kosher ("clean") food and not working on the Sabbath. Jesus often broke these rules, for example by healing infirm people on the Sabbath, something which was considered "work." Jesus did not oppose ritual purity but believed that observance of these rules was not enough (Matt 15:17–20). Jesus taught instead that inner purity and virtues, such as patience, humility, love, and mercy, were what God desired from people and that these virtues were more important than the laws of ritual purity (Matt 9:10–13; 22:23). Jesus was not outside the Jewish tradition in his opinion. Hundreds of years earlier, Jewish prophets had also encouraged virtue and denounced corrupt leaders and empty, formal ritual (Zech 7:8–10; Ezek 34; Amos 5:21–22; Mic 3:1–7).

However, many of the Jewish leaders rejected his teachings and considered him a bad influence and a false prophet because they believed that maintaining ritual purity was supremely important. Ritual purity also served to separate religiously observant Jews from sinful Jews and pagan idol worshippers. In addition to his brilliant teaching, Jesus was able to perform extraordinary miracles. The Jewish leaders could not explain how someone whom they considered a false prophet had such astonishing power. They concluded that Jesus was either demon possessed and derived his power from the devil, or that he was a magician who used sorcery to deceive people (Luke 11:15; John 7:12; 10:19). These accusations made against Jesus by Jewish leaders during his lifetime are preserved in the New Testament and are also reflected in later Jewish writings.

Today some popular political movements seem to look to Jesus for inspiration. Although he cared for the poor, outcasts and other marginalized people, Jesus' movement had no political objective or orientation. He preached repentance and spoke about the kingdom of God ("The kingdom of God is at hand. Repent."—Mark 1:15), but this was a call to inner conversion, not a call to arms or to create an earthly kingdom. "The kingdom of heaven is within you," he said (Luke 17:21). Social problems such as poverty and oppression would be solved or changed by one's own inner transformation, by changing personal values, attitudes, interactions and relationships, not by violence or revolution which he consistently opposed. "Whoever slaps you on your right cheek, turn the other to him also" (Matt 5:39) and "love your enemies" (Luke 6:35), he proclaimed. And yet, Jesus did not passively accept everyone regardless of their behavior. He did not condone sin, but he offered forgiveness to those who repented and changed their life.

People sometimes say that Jesus was a simply teacher or philosopher, or that Jesus considered himself to be merely a prophet. None of this is true. Jesus did not believe himself to be a prophet because Jewish prophets always preceded their statements with the words "Thus says the Lord" to show that their message was coming from God, not from the prophet (Isa 45:14; Amos 2:4). Jesus never said this phrase prior to offering his statements because he believed himself to *be* God, not a prophet or a teacher giving a message *from* God. He claimed for himself extraordinary authority: to forgive sins (Mark 2:10), change the Sabbath laws (Mark 2:28), to change the law of Moses and even the Ten Commandments (Matt 5:22), and he promised that he would return to judge the world (Matt 25:31–46).

Jesus often criticized wealthy and powerful Jews, including religious leaders, for their greed, hypocrisy, pride, corruption, and self-righteousness (Luke 16:14; Matt 23). They in turn rejected Jesus' actions and statements as "blasphemy" (words or actions dishonoring or insulting to God. Mark 2:8). They were alarmed by his great popularity among the masses and feared his growing influence. They had him arrested, hastily put on trial in the middle of the night and sentenced to death (Matt 26:65–66) the day before Passover, the second most important religious holiday of the year. However, because Judea was under Roman rule at that time, the Jewish leaders did not have the legal right to carry out the death penalty. Only the Roman governor, Pontius Pilate, could pronounce a death sentence and execute someone. But blasphemy was not a crime under Roman law and would not have warranted the death penalty by the Romans. The Jewish leaders believed that Jesus deserved death, so his "crime" was changed from "blasphemy" to "treason," a capital offense under Roman law (John 18:29–33). They told Pilate that Jesus claimed to be "King of the Jews" (Matt 27:11). In fact, Jesus had no political aspirations and when a crowd had tried to proclaim him king, he fled from them into the mountains (John 6:15).

Pontius Pilate sentenced Jesus to death by crucifixion, which was the most common form of execution at that time. The Roman world regarded crucifixion as the most painful, humiliating and degrading form of death. Jews assumed that any crucified person was rejected and cursed by God, and thus an additional motivation for having Jesus crucified was accomplished by the Jewish leaders: to completely discredit Jesus and his ideas. To this day, the primary reason why Jews reject Jesus as the Messiah is because he died on the cross. Jesus died on a Friday afternoon and most of his followers had gone into hiding upon his arrest. He was quickly buried because the Jewish Sabbath begins on Friday at sunset and no work, including a burial, can be performed on the Sabbath. Three days later, on Sunday morning, some female disciples returned to the tomb to finish the burial process only to find an empty tomb. Jesus appeared to them that morning alive in the flesh (Matt 28:1–10) and subsequently he appeared alive over the course of forty days to hundreds of disciples, not merely a handful (1 Cor 15:5–7). This is what Christians call the "resurrection" and they celebrate this event at Pascha, also known as Easter. These eyewitnesses to the resurrection were called "apostles" in the early church and they are the foundational source of information about the person, life, death and resurrection of Jesus. Today the term "apostle" is usually used only for the twelve closest disciples, but in the early church hundreds of people were eyewitnesses to the resurrection and were referred to as "apostles." The resurrection is discussed in greater detail in a different chapter of this book.

The Birth of Jesus and the "Lost Years"

One popular area of modern speculation about the life of Jesus concerns his so-called "lost years." Nothing is recorded about his life between his infancy and the start of his public ministry at age thirty, except for one incident when he was twelve years old (Luke 2:41–52). Jesus was born to a virgin mother, Mary. She was engaged to be married to a carpenter, Joseph, but while she was awaiting their marriage, she received a visit from an angel who told her that she would conceive a child who would be the Messiah and the Son of God. She asked how this was possible since she was a virgin and she was told that the child would be conceived by the power of the Holy Spirit. She accepted this as the will of God (Luke 1:26–31). Christian teaching is that Jesus has no human father. This is called the "virgin birth" even though it is really about the conception of Jesus. Joseph was also told about this remarkable conception in a dream and, being a devout and holy man, he accepted this as the will of God and he married Mary (Matt 1:18–24). Everyone assumed that Joseph was Jesus' biological father. Joseph helped to raise Jesus and provided a home and support for him and Mary. For Jews in those days, "marriage" was not a ceremony but consisted simply of the groom escorting the bride to his home. According to ancient Christian tradition, Joseph was much older than Mary, and was a widower with his own children, one of whom was James, called in the early church the "brother of the Lord." Mary and Joseph did not have their own children together but Mary remained a virgin dedicated to God.

Because nothing else is known about Jesus' early years, many people love to speculate about where he was or what he was doing during this time. Among the more popular proposals is that he travelled, perhaps to India, Persia or Egypt, to study philosophy or spirituality. And yet, absolutely no evidence exists that he ever left Palestine and no hint of influence from other cultures or religions are found in his teachings. As a rabbi, Jesus stood squarely within the Jewish tradition, even though he challenged it.

So why was nothing written about those years and what was Jesus doing then? First, we must realize the primary source of information about Jesus, writings called "the gospels," are not biographies. They were never intended to cover his entire life. They only tell us about his public ministry because this is the important period of Jesus' life and contain his teachings, his miracles, his crucifixion and resurrection. Nothing unusual or extraordinary occurred during Jesus' youth. He was growing up and preparing for his future ministry. He was raised by Mary and Joseph, worked as a carpenter and waited until the age of thirty to begin his ministry, the age at which one was considered a fully mature adult.

He performed no miracles, and gave no sermons during his youth. There was nothing unusual or extraordinary about him. He lived a very ordinary life in a small village. We know this because when he began his ministry the people of his village were shocked and surprised by his profound teaching, charismatic preaching and surprising healing powers. They had known him for nearly his entire life. They knew his family and extended relatives. How was it possible that he had these extraordinary abilities (Mark 6:2–3)? This is also how we can be certain that the speculation that he went to "study abroad," so to speak, is incorrect and baseless. If he had gone away for a period of time, everyone in the village would know that. They would point to his absence from the village and say that he got his "powers" during those years that he was "missing." But Jesus never travelled outside of Palestine, which was why the sudden manifestation of his abilities was so unexplainable to the villagers.

How else do we know that he never studied in Egypt or India or elsewhere? Jesus was a Jew who ministered to other Jews. What he studied was the Torah, the Prophets, the Psalms, and other Jewish writings and teachings. This was what was important to him as a rabbi. What would he possibly learn from idol worshippers? No Jew would ever go to places of idolatry to study and in fact, anyone who did so would have been shunned by other Jews.

Was Jesus Married?

Absolutely no evidence exists that Jesus was married, nor is there even a hint that he might have been married. Dan Brown's fictional book *The Da Vinci Code* seems to have popularized this idea in recent years. He claims that early Christian books were rejected by the church because they contained information that Jesus was married and even had a child. Many false books indeed were rejected by the church, not because they said that Jesus was married, but because they were falsified. Those false gospels (known as "apocrypha") were written in the late second and third centuries, long after eyewitnesses to Jesus life and teachings had died. A few years ago a tiny scrap of papyrus, literally the size of a business card, purportedly containing the words "Jesus" and "my wife" and was touted as the "Gospel of Jesus' Wife." It was quickly discredited as a forgery. Even the apocrypha do *not* say that Jesus was married. In fact, those false books were mostly composed by Gnostics, a group which arose in the second century and which denied the *humanity* of Christ. The Gnostic books did not say that Jesus was married and had a baby. Instead, Gnostics insisted on the *opposite*: that Jesus was not even human. He literally had no body, but was a divine being (called an "aeon") from the spirit realm. He only *seemed* human.

Part 2—Basic Issues That Confront Most Christians

The idea that Jesus was married but that this was "hidden" may seem reasonable to people today but it is incongruous with historical fact and would have been absolutely unnecessary. In the first centuries of Christianity, the church was not fighting to preserve the *divinity* of Christ but the *humanity* of Christ. This is the opposite of what we would expect today. The Greco-Roman mythologies had many stories about gods who came to earth and appeared in certain forms, such as a tree, or a deer or a person. But these gods never actually *became* a tree, a deer or a person. It was an illusion. This is what some people, mostly the Gnostics, were saying about Jesus. Gnostics liked the idea of Jesus as a god, his wise teachings and his miracles, but they could not believe that a god would become a human being, and especially that a god would die on the cross. So instead, Gnostics said that Jesus only *seemed* to be a human being and only *appeared* to have a body. They denied that he was human, that he was born, got tired, thirsty, had a body, suffered, or died on the cross. This idea was called "Docetism" (which means "to seem" or "to appear") and *this* was what the church was fighting against in the early centuries of Christianity: the denial of the *humanity* of Jesus. If Jesus had been married, and especially if he had a child, this would have been wonderful for the early church to prove to Gnostics that he was truly human. Christians would have had no reason to deny that he was married.

The woman most commonly linked to Jesus as a wife is Mary Magdalene, his most famous female disciple. But both in the Bible and in writings outside of the Bible not the slightest hint exists that she was anything other than a disciple. When she addresses him, she calls him "Rabboni" ("Teacher"—John 20:16), not "husband" or anything that would suggest a romantic or marriage relationship. Other relatives of Jesus, such as his mother, were known and mentioned in the Bible. It would have been perfectly natural for apostles or the Bible to mention a wife if Jesus had been married.

Some people make an "argument from silence." The Bible does not say whether Jesus was married and since most people *did* get married, Jesus *must* have been married. This is an illogical argument. Even today most people marry, but we all know people who have *never* been married. Since most people today marry, does this prove that people whom we think never married in fact must have been married? Of course not. Others say that Judaism required people to marry. But in the Bible itself, we see prophets and holy men who committed their lives to God and never married, such as John the Baptist and the prophet Jeremiah. The Jews did not force people to marry. Jesus chose not to marry because his purpose was not to have an ordinary life, to marry and have children like most people, but to do the work that God the Father had sent him to do. Still others point to practices in Orthodox Judaism as proof that Jesus must have been married, because this is the most conservative and traditional form of Judaism today and Orthodox Jewish men marry young. But this means nothing. There are countless practices in Judaism today which were not practiced during biblical times, including well-known traditions such as a Bar Mitzvah.

Other people say that the church hid Jesus' marriage because sex is somehow incompatible with holiness or that this would mean that he cannot be God. But marriage is God-given. Marriage is not a sin and sex within marriage has never been a sin. Perhaps the most compelling argument against the idea that Jesus was married is the fact that there would be no reason for the first Christians to hide the fact that Jesus was married, if he had been. Christians would have been accustomed to thinking of Jesus as a married man, just as they are accustomed today to think of him as a single man. In fact, he would have probably been considered the ideal married man. Not only would there have been no *reason* to hide the fact that Jesus was married, but such a fact could *not* have been suppressed. No super-structured church organization existed to determine what information was acceptable, what should be taught and what should be suppressed. The church consisted of individual congregations held together by a common beliefs about Jesus the Christ, not ruled by some powerful, remote centralized authority. The source of information about Jesus came from the hundreds of apostles who travelled freely and widely throughout the Roman Empire. No one could control what they said about Jesus and no one tried to. The apostles simply taught what they knew about Jesus, what they had seen and heard. If he had been married, no one could or would have hidden that fact.

Did Jesus Even Exist?

Even the mere existence of Jesus as a historical person has been rejected by some people. Anything can be rejected on the basis of insufficient "proof." There are also people who deny that the moon landings or the Jewish Holocaust ever occurred. Most of us would consider such people ignorant or irrational. Clearly, we cannot demand "proofs" of Jesus' existence in the form of photographs or film. We must look to other types of evidence to confirm events and claims from antiquity. Conclusions must be based on logical inference or details which corroborate documents. Religious texts, such as the books of the New Testament, are valuable historical documents in their own right and should not be dismissed outright simply because they are written with a faith perspective. All authors have a point of view and no one is completely impartial or unbiased, whether the book is religious, historical, political, philosophical, psychological, etc. Having a point of view does not render everything in a book false or unhistorical.

Jesus definitely existed as a historical person. In fact, more independent evidence exists for Jesus than for the existence of Socrates, Homer, Abraham, Moses, and many other important historical figures whose existence people would never think to question. Evidence of Jesus' existence is found both in Christian documents (the New Testament) and outside the Christian tradition in Roman and Jewish writings.

Was the Historical Jesus a Construct of Mythology?

In recent years people have rejected Christian claims about Jesus by saying that his story was just copied from other mythologies at the time. Such false statements are easily concocted, and proliferate on the internet as they are quickly and endlessly repeated. But the *slightest* research reveals that those assertions are not true. Some so-called "similarities" are so broad that they cannot be fairly considered "similarities" because they are merely titles and images common in many religions, such as "Son of God" or comparisons to light or the sun. But even in that case, one might fairly ask, if something false exists, does that mean that the truth does not exist? Because "fool's gold" (pyrite) exists does this mean that actual gold does *not* exist? The fact that those mythologies were false, does not prove that statements about Jesus are also false.

One well-known "fact" cited to "prove" that Jesus is the product of mythology is that Jesus was not born on December 25. The actual date of Jesus' birth is unknown because people did not celebrate birthdays and often did not know their own birthdates. December 25 was deliberately chosen by the Christian church for the celebration of Christ's birth, with the full knowledge that he was not born on that date. That date was chosen in the fourth century not because details of Christ's birth or life were drawn from mythology but to respond to pagan claims. Pagan gods did have "birthdays" and the "birthdays" of some of the most popular pagan gods who were being worshipped during the fourth century fell on or around December 25, including Sol Invictus (Invincible Sun) and Mithras, also considered a god of light. That time of year is near the winter solstice and pagan Romans worshipped light and the sun. By choosing December 25 as the birthday of Christ, the church was not drawing its teachings from mythology. Instead it was making a profound protest against idolatry, against the worship of an object, the sun, and making a statement that Jesus Christ alone is the light of the world and the true sun of righteousness.

Some claim that Christians simply copied ideas from various myths, such as the "virgin birth," and that many similar stories existed in antiquity. In the context of this chapter we cannot discuss every accusation, however, let us consider that claim. People assert, as a similarity, that other gods were also said to be products of a "virgin birth," such as Mithras and Horus. But Mithras was "born" out of a stone and Horus was conceived by his mother, Isis, after his father, Osiris, was murdered and Osiris' body parts were scattered. Isis painstakingly retrieved the pieces of her husband's body except for Osiris' penis. She was able to use magic to create a penis out of gold and thus she conceived Horus. The goddess Athena was "born" when Zeus had a headache and his head was cracked open with an axe to relieve the pain. Out popped Athena, completely grown and dressed in full armor. This would also be considered a "virgin birth." None of these mythologies, nor any others, bear any similarity to the birth of Jesus, nor did they inspire stories about the birth of Jesus. These are just three examples of many false comparisons between the historical Jesus and mythologies which are being enthusiastically circulated on the internet in order to discredit Christianity. Accounts of the birth of Jesus were written during the first century, during the lifetimes of people who knew Jesus and his mother. In fact, a great deal of difference exists between the life of Jesus and various figures from mythology. The most radical and monumental difference is also the most important: only Jesus was a real, *historical* person and only his life and deeds are corroborated in historical records.

The Jewish Reality

Some say it is logical, even rational, that Jesus' followers drew these stories about him from mythology, that they were inspired to say that he was the Son of God because of the pagan culture, or that they decided on a whim to continue to "follow" him even after his crucifixion. But this is *not* rational.

Part 2—Basic Issues That Confront Most Christians

We must remember that all of the first followers of Jesus were Jews. They did not call themselves "Christians" until decades later. They did not believe they were abandoning Judaism to embrace a new religion, certainly not one which was inspired by idol-worshippers and pagan mythology. The followers of Jesus were simply Jews who believed that the Messiah had come and he was Jesus of Nazareth. Nothing else differentiated them from other Jews, not their core beliefs, practices, lifestyle, appearance, etc. No one expected the Messiah to be the Son of God, so they did not believe that he is the Son of God because they believed him to be the Messiah. Rather, it was what they had *experienced* in the person of Jesus, his own words about himself and his deeds, especially the resurrection, which convinced them that he was both Messiah and Lord.

Jesus was neither the first nor the last person believed to be the messiah by Jews. The most famous false messiah was Simon bar Kokhba, who led a revolt against the Roman Empire in the second century. And yet no followers or movement remain from Simon bar Kokhba or those other "messiahs" of the past. Why is Jesus different? Because of who he was and what he did. His followers did not "invent" ideas about him. They came to conclusions about who he was because of what they had personally experienced, day after day after day. Not a few or twelve or a hundred, but thousands of Jews who personally knew Jesus were compelled to the unavoidable conclusion that he was not simply the Messiah but also the Lord. These were not Jews who had left Judaism for something else, but Jews who were committed to their religion. The conclusion they reached about Jesus was such a departure from what would be expected of Jews that it must be acknowledged from a purely objective standpoint that Jesus must have been extremely remarkable and extraordinary. Stories about Jesus were not invented by these devout Jews but truly reflect their *experience* of Jesus, an experience so intense, dramatic and profound that it changed them forever.

Why invent a Messiah? Why call anyone other than God, "the Lord"? It is unthinkable for a Jew. The thousands of followers of Jesus did not suddenly and collectively become delusional. No: They simply could not deny what they knew to be true from their own personal experience. If they were going to "invent" a Messiah, they certainly would not have chosen a poor rabbi from Nazareth whom other Jews considered a failure and cursed by God because he died by crucifixion.

Jewish Writings

An important source for the existence of the historical Jesus is a first-century Jewish historian, Flavius Josephus, who wrote around the year 90 CE.[1] Josephus mentions Jesus' extraordinary teaching, his miracles, that the Jewish leaders conspired against him, that he was crucified under Pilate and that the followers of Jesus (whom Josephus calls "the tribe of the Christians") were still around when Josephus was writing. Josephus was Jewish, so he was not promoting Christianity. Josephus not only discusses Jesus, but also mentions John the Baptist and James, son of Joseph and the head of the church in Jerusalem. James and John the Baptist are mentioned in the New Testament, just as Jesus is found in the New Testament. Would these two men be real, historical people, whose existence is confirmed in the writings of Josephus, but Jesus alone be a total fiction?

What about the miracles of Jesus? Today is easy for people to be skeptical and say that Christians simply invented the miracle stories. But no Jewish writings, including the most critical Jewish references to Jesus, ever denied that Jesus performed remarkable signs and miracles. Josephus mentions Jesus' miracles and Jesus is denounced in the Talmud, an ancient collection of Jewish teaching compiled around the fifth century. Although the Talmud is not from the first century and contains no historical information about Jesus, it does preserve Jewish criticisms of him from later centuries. Some people believe that these comments are not about Jesus, but the similarities are compelling. The person's name is "Yeshu."[2] He was from Nazareth, had disciples, is described as a "sorcerer," and was "hanged" on the eve of the Passover.[3] Other passages from the Talmud also reference Yeshu as someone who practiced magic[4] and yet other passages relate people praying to Yeshu for healings which the Talmud explains as magic or sorcery.[5] Even though the Talmud rejects Jesus as the Messiah, these statements are very significant. It is obvious that if Jesus had never performed miracles, which were important to Christians to prove that he fulfilled messianic prophecies, Jewish writers would have denied that he

---

1. Josephus, *Antiquities of the Jews*.

2. "Jesus" in Hebrew.

3. Sanhedrin 43a. Neusner, *Babylonian Talmud*, 16:220. The Jews consider crucifixion a form of hanging.

4. "Jesus the Nazarene practiced magic and led Israel astray." Sotah 47a; Sanhedrin 107b. Neusner, *Babylonian Talmud*, 11:239; 16:578.

5. Schäfe, *Jesus in the Talmud*.

ever performed signs and wonders. But no ancient Jewish writers ever denied that Jesus did miracles. They denied that his power came from God, but that he performed amazing signs and wonders is incontrovertible and stands unopposed in ancient writings.

Roman Historians

Two Roman historians from the late first/early second centuries, Tacitus and Suetonius, also have references to Jesus. Tacitus reports Nero's persecution of Christians and remarks that Jesus was executed by crucifixion under the Roman governor of Judea, Pontius Plate.[6] We no longer have the Roman records, but they had the records. Nero's persecution took place only about thirty years after the time of Jesus. Pontius Pilate was well known and his activities would have been a matter of record. No first-century Romans or Jews ever suggested that Christians were worshipping someone who never existed. Rather, Christians were mocked for their devotion to a crucified criminal. Tacitus disparages Christians and certainly has no bias in favor of Christianity. Suetonius used the Roman imperial archives to research his history of the Caesars. His reference to Jesus is indirect, but a compelling corroboration nonetheless. Suetonius reports that the Emperor Claudius expelled the Jews from the city of Rome because of "disturbances" among the Jews in Rome over "Chrestus."[7] Many scholars believe that this is a reference to heated arguments in the synagogues over whether Jesus was the "Christos," the Greek word for "Messiah."[8] Claudius expelled the Jews of Rome in the year 49 CE. This would have been only about fifteen years after the death and resurrection of Jesus.

Arguments about whether Jesus was the Messiah had been dividing Jews all over the Roman world. If Jesus had never existed this fact would have come out and been spread among the Jewish synagogues. Certainly Jews would not be arguing about whether he was the Messiah in the years immediately following his death and resurrection if he had never existed. At this time, there were still hundreds of Jesus' followers who were eyewitnesses to

---

6. Tacitus, *Annals*, 15.44.
7. Suetonius, "Life of Claudius," 25.4.
8. The "e" of "Chrestus" and "i" of "Christos" would have been pronounced the same in Greek. During the first century, the common language of the Roman Empire, even in the city of Rome was Greek, not Latin. Hence, the arguments in the synagogue were about the "Christos," "the Christ." Suetonius Latinized the name by spelling it Chrestus.

his preaching and resurrection. These followers, the apostles, were bringing their message to their fellow Jews at synagogues throughout the Mediterranean area. Their message was simple: The Messiah has come, Jesus of Nazareth, who was not only the Messiah but the Lord himself. He had fulfilled the prophecies and he had been crucified, but he rose from the dead. This message was spread in synagogues throughout the empire by hundreds of eyewitnesses to Jesus' ministry. Not only were the apostolic eyewitnesses to Jesus still alive, even the Jewish leaders who had put Jesus to death were still alive. The claim that Jesus was the Messiah incited massive debates in first-century Judaism. But no Jew ever questioned Jesus' existence or even his miracles. The only question for Jews was whether the Messiah could be this crucified rabbi.

Some people ask, if Jesus existed, why was his trial not recorded by Roman historians or why is Jesus mostly absent from Roman historical records? First, no one knew how important Jesus would become later in history. Many now-famous people were relatively obscure during their lifetimes, such as Wolfgang Mozart or Vincent van Gogh, but they were known in their circles of influence and activity. Jesus was well known to Jews in Judea and Galilee during the years of his ministry because he was a religious leader. He would not have been noticed by the Romans because they had no interest in Jewish preachers or rabbis and his was not a political movement. He was not a threat to Roman order. Jesus eventually did come to the attention of the Romans when the Jewish leaders brought him to the Roman governor, Pontius Pilate, for trial on a charge of treason. But he was not "important" or a noteworthy figure to the Romans at the time of his death. The Romans executed countless people in their vast empire on the slightest suspicion of treason. To the Romans, Jesus was nothing special. Jesus' importance in world history grew *after* his death. This is why nothing was written about him during his lifetime. Roman historians would never have written about a poor Jewish rabbi in a faraway corner of the empire who died on a cross. Romans valued prestige, power, wealth and status. Jesus had none of those. Hence, he was nothing to the Romans.

Tacitus, a pagan Roman, and Josephus, a Jew, confirm two basic and incontrovertible facts about Jesus in the New Testament: that he died by crucifixion under Pilate and that he had followers. Would these historians, a Jew and a Roman, writing independently of each other, in different places and different times, conspire to promote a "mythological" figure, Jesus? Were these highly educated and intelligent historians fooled? In fact and in deed, Jesus existed and *no one* in antiquity—those living closest to the historical time period—ever denied or even questioned that fact.

The Gospels

Most of the historical information about Jesus comes from the gospels: first-century accounts of his public ministry, death and resurrection attributed to Matthew, Mark, Luke and John. The exact date of the composition of the gospels is unknown. Most biblical scholars date them between approximately 65 and 90 CE, but they could be earlier. Some people argue that if Jesus' ministry ended around 33 CE, the gospels are too late to be reliable sources of information about Jesus decades later. After all, the average human lifespan was considerably shorter in the first century. It is true that the average lifespan was shorter, however, the key word is "average." Many infants and children did not survive and women frequently did not survive their childbearing years. This fact skews the "average." Although they were exposed to more germs, people also developed stronger immunities. They had a natural and active lifestyle and they were not killed by unnatural causes such as car crashes. Many people lived well into their seventies and eighties in antiquity, and some even past the age of one hundred. Hundreds of people were eyewitnesses to Jesus and at the time the gospels were written there were certainly many who were still alive, some thirty, forty, fifty and even sixty years later. This would be comparable to countless people alive today who remember the Vietnam War, which ended over forty years ago, President Kennedy's assassination, over fifty years ago, or World War II from more than seventy years ago. Just as significant events are remembered by each of us vividly, such as the Kennedy assassination, those eyewitnesses of Jesus would have vividly remembered what he said and did, particularly if they had followed him as a disciple. They did not hear him preach once or twice but countless times. Doubtless, like many preachers and others who speak frequently, such as politicians, Jesus had certain stories and sayings he would tell over and over to his audience, like a modern day "stump speech" or "talking points." These lessons would have been easily remembered by his followers, just as we easily remember well-known family stories which are repeated by relatives at our gatherings. The transmission of Jesus' teachings by his followers is not like the "telephone game," in which a disciple heard the message once and tried to recall it years later. This is why the apostles, as eyewitnesses to what Jesus said and did, were so important. They had spent a great deal of time with Jesus and knew his life and teachings *very* well.

People sometimes question why Jesus' teachings were not immediately written down. There are two reasons for this: First, the disciples believed that Jesus would return very, very soon. But the second reason is more important: People did not get information from writings but from talking to each other. There were no newspapers. Books were expensive and rare. Many people did not read at all. But even if they did, books were considered *less* reliable than oral teaching. This is difficult for us to understand today because we rely on writing and we put more trust in writing. But the opposite was the case in antiquity. Back then, all books were *hand* copied. You never knew whether the book you were reading was actually by the person who was the supposed author or whether the copyist had copied it accurately. People could easily distort a book when they copied it by adding their own comments or removing what they did not agree with. Sometimes people maliciously altered books to discredit their enemies or even wrote entirely false books which they claimed were written by an enemy, hoping that the contents would bring shame and disgrace to their foe.

The first Christians relied on "oral tradition," passing down the sayings and stories about Jesus orally. This was not unreliable, nor did people consider oral teaching unreliable. People in antiquity were accustomed to learning lessons just by listening and memorizing. There were no "textbooks" since books were rare and expensive. Furthermore, they trusted oral teaching because they knew their teacher and their teacher's qualifications. The qualification for "apostles," was that they were eyewitnesses to what Jesus said and did.

Chronological Snobbery

Occasionally people are dismissive of any historical Christian claims on the basis that people who lived long ago were much more prone to accept anything they were told. This intellectually indefensible. The assumption that people who lived in the past were foolish, less intelligent, or more gullible simply because they did not have technology has been dubbed "chronological snobbery." How can it be true that people who lived in the past were less intelligent? How arrogant it is to think that we alone are intelligent! The ancient Greeks produced countless intellectual luminaries in science, mathematics, philosophy, literature and medicine, not to mention remarkable architectural and artistic marvels. How did they construct the Parthenon without cranes and without calculators? What about Roman engineering? The Romans knew how to pour concrete underwater and create artificial harbors. They brought water from miles away via aqueducts and built the Colosseum, all without "technology." Today, we are not even sure *how* they were able to do these things without the tools that we take for granted. It is nonsensical to assert that humans were less intelligent before the advent of technology. One could argue that the ancients were *more* intelligent since they were capable of such accomplishments without technology. If people during the time of Christ were at least as intelligent as we are, then it follows that we cannot dismiss Christian claims or the existence of Jesus on the basis that people who lived long ago were ignorant, stupid and gullible.

Indirect Confirmation

Even though it is impossible to "prove" the existence and divinity of Christ, indirect confirmation of the veracity of the gospels exists and should be taken into consideration before dismissing Christian claims. It is illogical and unreasonable to expect Christians to produce the kinds of "proof" of Jesus that would satisfy modern critics. One of the challenges of "documenting" Jesus and much of ancient history is that most of the writings which existed in antiquity have been lost. Nonetheless, some surprising evidence exists to prove the reliability of the New Testament. For example, the earliest known reference to Jesus may be an obscure statement by a first-century Greek historian who was challenging Christianity. Today, his statements actually indirectly confirm the New Testament and a key event at the time of the crucifixion. The historian was Thallos, who wrote a three-volume history of the eastern Mediterranean around the year 55 CE. Although that work has been lost, we know that Thallos discussed Jesus and his crucifixion because Julius Africanus (a third-century Christian author) quoted from Thallos in Julius' own work, called *History of the World*, written around 220 CE. Although Julius' work has also been lost, it had been quoted by a Byzantine historian, George Syncellus, around 800 CE, in his work called *Chronicle*. That book has survived. Syncellus quotes Julius' discussion of the darkness which covered the earth while Christ was on the cross, a detail described in the gospels. Thallos was disputing the fact that the darkness which occurred on that day was supernatural and claimed that the darkness was simply due to a solar eclipse. After checking the astronomical records,

Julius responded that there was no eclipse that year and that no eclipse lasts for three hours (the period of time that Jesus was on the cross). What is extraordinarily important about this discussion is that Thallos, writing only about twenty years after Christ's crucifixion, was trying to explain the strange darkness which occurred while Christ was on the cross. At the time Thallos was writing, that was a relatively recent historical occurrence. Thallos does not disagree *that* the inexplicable darkness occurred. He only disputes the *cause*. This serves as independent corroboration that darkness in fact actually did cover the earth for three hours on the day of Christ's death, supporting this detail of the gospel narrative (Mark 15:33).[9]

Another detail from the life of Christ which indirectly substantiates the gospels is the existence of the famous "star of Bethlehem." Jesus was probably born around the year 6 BCE. (He was born during the reign of King Herod the Great, who died in 4 BCE. Our modern dates, based on the date of Jesus' birth were created during the Middle Ages and the date arrived at for Jesus' birth was off by a few years). According to the gospel of Matthew, magi (Persian astronomers) came from the east to find the baby who had been born "King of the Jews" (Matt 2:1–2). They knew this from the appearance of a celestial sight which we call today the "star of Bethlehem." Ancient people were fascinated by stars and spent a great deal of time studying them. They were familiar with the appearance of the sky throughout the year and any change in the sky was believed to be significant. The ancients thought that planets were "wandering stars." Planets shine in the sky like stars, but have orbits since they are planets. Because their orbits are elliptical, distances between planets vary and at times they seem to come very close together in the sky. This is called a "conjunction." In the year 6 BCE, the planets Jupiter and Saturn seemed to come together three times that year in what is called a "triple conjunction."[10] Jupiter was called the "king" star, because it was named for the king of the gods, Jupiter, and Saturn was considered the star of the Jews because the Jewish holy day is Saturday, the seventh day of the week, which is named for the god Saturn. This conjunction happens only every 140 years and it was unusual enough to attract the attention of the magi. They easily concluded from this celestial sign that a King (Jupiter) of the Jews (Saturn) was to be born.

---

9. Syncellus, *Chronography of George Synkellos*.
10. "Astronomer's Explanation for the Star of Bethlehem," *Science 2.0*.

Part 2 — Basic Issues That Confront Most Christians

The Divinity of Jesus

Christians believe that Jesus is not only human but divine. He is the Son of God who became a human being to live with us, to teach us, to love us, to show us who God is and what it truly means to be human. This, of course, is a matter of faith, not something which can be "proven." While some people claim that Christians "invented" the divinity of Jesus later, in fact the first Jewish followers of Jesus came to the conclusion that he was no mere human (Mark 5:35–41). During his lifetime, Jesus exhibited extraordinary powers, not simply power over disease, infirmities, and evil spirits, but also powers over nature, such as stilling a storm, walking on water, etc. The greatest power he had was power over life and death, when he raised people from the dead and rose from the dead himself. He knew also the future and could read thoughts.

"Jesus is Lord" is one of the earliest statements of faith made about Jesus, but these first followers of Jesus were not "Christians." That word did not even exist and the religion did not suddenly spring into existence after the resurrection. The Jesus movement was a sect within Judaism for decades until Jesus believers were finally rejected by the rest of Judaism. These first Jesus believers were all *Jews*. Today scholars call them "Jewish-Christians" because they were Jews who believed that Jesus was the Messiah (the "Christ"). Other than that, they were no different from any other Jews. They did not cease being Jews, living like Jews or thinking like Jews. They simply believed that the Messiah had come, and it was the Lord himself who had come to earth as Jesus of Nazareth. They did not need to "invent" the divinity of Jesus to support their "new religion." They did not *have* a "new" religion and they were not intending to start one. They were, and they remained, devout Jews. They would never have invented the idea of Jesus being God if they had not personally *experienced* something utterly extraordinary in their personal interactions with him.

Writer Reza Aslan, in his book *Zealot: The Life and Times of Jesus of Nazareth*, distorts Jesus' life and message. Among his claims is that Saul of Tarsus, later known as Paul, invented the idea of Jesus' divinity to appeal to pagans. But Saul himself had been a devout Jew. Why would he turn to apostasy and decide that Jesus was God? If he were the *first* follower of Jesus to suggest such a thing, he would have been denounced by the other members of the movement, since this was still a Jewish sect. It would have been impossible for Saul/Paul to "convince" other Jewish followers of Jesus that Jesus was God. But the fact is that Saul joined a movement that was well underway, and Saul had been an ardent *persecutor* of the followers of Jesus. Why? Because *they* taught that Jesus was the Lord. Saul did not invent that idea. The divinity of Jesus was part of the message of the church from the beginning. It was the very charge for which Jesus himself was condemned to death by the Jewish leaders and it was the very belief that caused the Jewish leaders, including Saul, to persecute the followers of Jesus and charge them with blasphemy. The followers of Jesus *already* believed that Jesus was God, for which Saul persecuted them. Claiming that your rabbi was the Messiah was not offensive nor was it blasphemy. But claiming that he was the Lord certainly was.

Some people assume that few, if any Jews, joined this sect of Judaism which would eventually become "Christianity" and that it immediately grew among the pagans. But this is incorrect and is not supported by the historical record. *All* of the first followers of Jesus were Jews and the movement spread through the hundreds of synagogues of the Jews in diaspora (Jews who spoke Greek and lived outside of Palestine). One of the reasons why the Jesus movement spread so quickly was that there were millions of Jews in diaspora. Every Sabbath, the hundreds of apostles travelling throughout the Roman Empire visited those synagogues and talked about Jesus. They shared their personal experiences of Jesus with their fellow Jews and opened up the Scriptures to prove that Jesus fulfilled the prophecies. Thousands and thousands of Jews became followers of Jesus. Slowly, pagans also became interested in the movement and joined it. Since Jews were a minority in the Roman Empire, eventually the number of former pagans who accepted Jesus outnumbered the Jews. But for decades, the movement had been a Jewish sect. The followers of Jesus were not trying to appeal to the pagans by "making" Jesus into a "god."

Some would argue that if indeed the first followers of Jesus were Jews, it is impossible that they would have accepted the divinity of Jesus. No Jew would ever accept that, so someone must have "invented" the divinity of Jesus later. But these Jewish followers of Jesus *did* believe and teach that Jesus was the Lord because of what they *experienced* in the person of Jesus Christ. They could not deny who and what he was. Today, most of us think of religious faith as something to which we must intellectually assent: "I accept this set of beliefs" or "I can intellectually agree with these concepts." Religion seems to be a set of ideas or mental concepts to be accepted or rejected. But the first followers of Jesus were not asked to accept a set of beliefs or statements. They were simply devout Jews who met a certain charismatic rabbi from Nazareth. As they followed him, watched him and grew to know him they slowly began to understand who he was: first a rabbi, then the Messiah, and later the Lord himself. Christians always taught both the divinity and the humanity of Jesus because both were present and obvious in his life and ministry. It was not an extraordinary conclusion for them because they *experienced* Jesus. They experienced someone who was completely human—he was born, grew up, was thirsty, tired, hungry, bled, died—and someone who at the same time was completely divine—he knew the future, knew people's thoughts, had complete power over life, death, sickness, spirits, etc. They did not have to "decide" what to believe about him: they knew who and what he was because they knew *him*.

4

The Resurrection of Jesus Christ

Eugenia Constantinou

What Is the Resurrection?

THE RESURRECTION OF JESUS Christ is the foundation of the Christian faith. Jesus had been condemned to death by the Jewish leaders on a charge of blasphemy, but since the Jews were under Roman occupation they did not have the right to execute anyone. It was necessary to bring Jesus before the Roman governor of Judea, Pontius Pilate, who sentenced Jesus to death by crucifixion. Almost all of Jesus' disciples were hiding, afraid that they too would be arrested by the Jewish leaders, put on trial and sentenced to death as Jesus had been. Jesus died on a Friday afternoon and was buried quickly. Jews observe the Sabbath from sunset Friday until sunset Saturday and no work is permitted during that time. Due to the short time frame between the time of his death around 3:00 pm and the time of sunset around 6:00 pm, Jesus' female followers were not able to complete the Jewish burial procedures, which consisted of washing and anointing the body with spices and ointments. The body was hurriedly taken down from the cross, covered with a linen shroud and placed in a new tomb. The entrance to the tomb, a cave-like chamber hewn out of the side of a hill, was closed up with a large rock. Then his disciples departed to observe the Sabbath and the feast of Passover. While he was alive, Jesus had predicted his resurrection (John 2:19; Matt 27:62; Mark 9:31; 10:34; Luke 18:33). Thinking that Jesus' disciples might steal the body and claim that he rose from the dead, the Jewish leaders asked Pilate to seal the tomb and assign a contingent of soldiers to guard it (Matt 27:63–33). At dawn on Sunday morning, Jesus' female disciples came to the tomb to finish the burial process but the tomb was empty

(Matt 28; Mark 16; Luke 24; John 20) except for the linen shroud that had been used to cover the body and the cloth used to hold the mouth closed (John 20: 5–7). The distraught women feared that someone had stolen the body, but angels appeared to them and told them that Jesus had risen from the dead (Matt 28:2–7; Mark 16:5–6; Luke 24:4–10). As they ran to tell the other disciples, Jesus himself appeared to the women (Matt 28:9–10; John 20:15–18). Later male disciples came to see the empty tomb for themselves and confirmed that the tomb was empty (Luke 24:22–14) but the grave cloths had been left behind (John 20:3–8). Jesus appeared physically to his disciples that day and on many more occasions over the next forty days. The day of resurrection is celebrated as "Pascha" by Orthodox Christians, and called "Easter" by other Christians.

For Orthodox Christians, the most important aspect of Jesus' life is not his death on the cross but his resurrection from the dead. This is what is emphasized in Orthodox theology, prayers, hymns, etc. The death of Christ on the cross was not something that God the Father demanded or required to satisfy some sense of "justice" because someone had to "pay the price" for sin. Rather the death of Christ on the cross is the ultimate expression of God's love. Because Christ was sinless and because he was God, the creator and giver of life, death could not keep him in the grave.

The resurrection is important because Orthodox Christianity is not a belief system or a set of ethical principles. It is the offer of eternal life in union with God. All of us live subject to the reality of death. God did not create death. Death is *un*natural since we were not created to die. And yet, we do die because we all sin. Death is the consequence of sin because God is the source of life. When we choose to do something that takes us away from God (committing a sin) then we are choosing death. Christ destroyed the power of death, conquering death by rising from the dead. If Jesus did not rise, he is nothing more than a failed messiah, a promising rabbi whose life met an unfortunate end.

The Historical Basis for the Resurrection

The bodily resurrection of Jesus has strong historical attestation in the New Testament.[1] All four gospels testify to this event as well as the letters of Paul, especially 1 Corinthians (1 Cor 15). All of the accounts of Christ's resurrection are simple, straightforward and unembellished, not exaggerated

1. See ch. 3 for a discussion on the historical reliability of the Gospels.

or heavily laden with religious overtones. They describe an event. The oldest written account of the resurrection appearances of Christ can be found in a letter addressed to the Christian community in Corinth, Greece around the year 53. Paul cites the resurrection appearances of Jesus (1 Cor 15:3–8), including one occasion when Jesus appeared to a large gathering of over five hundred people (1 Cor 15:6). Eye witnesses of the resurrection were called "apostles" in the early church. Today the term "apostle" is usually reserved for Jesus' inner circle of twelve followers, and sometimes people think that Jesus only had twelve disciples. But Jesus had thousands of disciples during his earthly ministry and hundreds of apostles who were eyewitnesses of the resurrection. The apostles were extremely important in the early church because they had personally known Jesus, followed him during his earthly ministry and they had seen him alive again after his death on the cross. After the resurrection, the apostles travelled widely throughout the Roman Empire telling people about Jesus. What is most significant about Paul's comments to the Corinthians is that at the time he wrote to the Corinthians, most of the eyewitnesses were still alive and he points to that fact. Many of the apostles had passed through Corinth, a significant port city, and certainly others would as well. The apostles did not stay in Judea but travelled widely. Paul was reminding the Corinthians that there were many, many eyewitnesses to the resurrection and by this he implied that anyone could question the apostles about their experience of the resurrected Christ.

Some people dismiss the eyewitness accounts of the resurrection by saying that the resurrection was invented by the followers of Jesus to give their "new religion" legitimacy or to bolster their claim that Jesus was the Messiah. But the followers of Jesus were all devout Jews. They were not interested in starting a "new religion." The Jesus movement was part of Judaism for several decades before it became known as "Christianity" and the resurrection was the very first message ever proclaimed about Jesus, long before there was any hint that eventually this movement would break off from Judaism.

The undisputable reality is that the resurrection of Jesus cannot be dismissively explained away. A profound and undeniable experience changed the followers of Jesus. When Jesus died on Friday, his followers were mourning his death and hiding in terror. Jesus had been executed and they feared that they too would be arrested and put to death. But worst of all, their hopes had been dashed. They were convinced that he was the

Messiah but now he was dead and the movement was dead with him. But on Sunday morning, with the discovery of the empty tomb and Jesus' appearances to his followers, everything changed. They saw him alive again, hugged him, touched him, ate with him, and marveled at his wounds. There was no doubt. The formerly timid and frightened disciples burst out into the world with the most amazing message in the history of the world: that death is not the end. This is the essence of the gospel message: Jesus the Messiah had risen from the dead, and because of this, you too can have eternal life.

Arguments Raised Against the Resurrection

Jesus Never Actually Died

Some theorize that Jesus only seemed dead, but had recovered in the tomb and got out. This is impossible. Jesus was clearly dead. He was pierced in the heart with a spear by a Roman soldier (John 19:34) and the Roman governor, Pontius Pilate, released the body for burial (Matt 27:57–58; Mark 15:43–45; John 19:38; Luke 23:50–52). It is also impossible that someone could exit the tomb by himself. Jesus would have been extremely weak from his ordeal and the great loss of blood. The stone which blocked the entrance to the tomb weighed several tons and could not be moved by a single man, even one who was completely strong and healthy.

Jesus Was Never Buried

Crucifixion was designed to be the most horrific form of death. It was slow, painful, and intended to be a public humiliation. Ordinarily, the Romans left the bodies on the cross to rot until all that remained was a skeleton. Denying burial to a crucified man was part of the humiliation and horror of this form of execution. For this reason some people argue that Jesus was never buried. However, the Romans made many exceptions to ordinary Roman law and procedures in order to accommodate Jewish religious laws and sensibilities. Jewish law forbade anyone from hanging on the cross at night. The Romans accepted this and made sure that any Jew who had been crucified was dead before nightfall. They broke the legs of the two thieves who had been crucified with Jesus to hasten their death (John 19:31–32). In order to be sure that Jesus was dead a lance was put into his side, piercing the heart and the sack surrounding it (John 19:34). Jews also did not typically bury a condemned criminal in a family tomb. But one of Jesus' followers came forward, Joseph of Arimathea, who greatly respected Jesus and did not consider him a criminal. Joseph buried Jesus in a new tomb in which no one else had ever been buried (Matt 27:57–60; Mark 15:43–46; Luke 23:50–53; John 19:38–41).

The Disciples Saw a Ghost, Spirit or a Dream

This is impossible since all of the resurrection appearances emphasize that Jesus appeared to his disciples physically. They did not always immediately recognize him (Luke 24:13–16; John 20:11–16). The resurrected body of Jesus was not bound by time and space (Luke 24:30–31, 36; John 20:19, 26) and he seemed to take on a different appearance at times (Luke 24:13–26; John 20:15). But the disciples touched him and saw the wounds of his crucifixion (Luke 24:39–40; John 20:20, 27). He ate a piece of fish in their presence (Luke 24:41–43). He appeared to them during the day while they were awake and active. They were not dreaming (Matt 28:1, 9; Luke 24:1, 13–17.)

The Disciples Stole the Body

Jesus said that he would rise from the dead (John 2:19; Matt 27:62; Mark 9:31; 10:34; Luke 18:33) and the explanation given for the resurrection by the Jewish leaders, which still circulates today, is that Jesus' disciples stole his body. There are three problems with this theory. First, the burial cloths were left behind (John 20:5–7). No one would steal the body and leave the burial cloths behind. They would have to unwrap and carry a mangled, bloody body. Furthermore, it would have been extremely difficult to remove the burial cloth. The body of Jesus had numerous bloody wounds and the cloth would have stuck to the wounds when the blood dried. Second, why would the disciples steal the body? If Jesus never rose, then he was a liar, not the Messiah. Why would the disciples risk stealing the body, a very serious crime under Roman law, to defend or support a dead man, someone whom they had believed in but whose prediction of resurrection did not come true? The disciples had nothing to gain by stealing the body and everything to lose. Last, the Jewish leaders themselves ensured that no one could legitimately claim that Jesus' body was stolen because they themselves asked Pontius Pilate to set a guard outside the tomb (Matt 27:62–66).

Part 2—Basic Issues That Confront Most Christians

How could the massive stone be moved aside without waking any of the guards? Roman soldiers could not explain the absence of the body, so they were bribed to say they had fallen asleep and that the disciples had stolen the body (Matt 28:11–15). The penalty for falling asleep while on guard duty was death, so they would never have allowed themselves to fall asleep, but they could not explain the absence of the body, so they were paid for their silence and escaped with their own lives.

Jesus "Rose in Their Hearts"

The theory behind this common explanation is that the disciples of Jesus decided that they would "carry on" for Jesus after his death. They would say that he rose because he rose "spiritually," or he rose "in their hearts." The disciples never said this. He rose bodily, physically, and this is what they bore witness to. Some people say that the disciples wanted to continue the ministry of Jesus. They wanted to spread his message of peace and love, so they said that Jesus rose. But the consistent message in the New Testament, and the message of the disciples, was not "God loves you" or "Love your neighbor as yourself," or any other such thing. Other teachers, prophets and philosophers could preach a similar message and it does not require someone to have risen from the dead to give that message legitimacy. The apostles did not essentially preach an ethical message which most people today associate with Jesus. The "good news" brought by the apostles was that Jesus is the Messiah and the Lord. He was crucified but he rose from the dead and because of this, you too can have eternal life. The resurrection is foundational to that message. On the very first occasion when Peter preached to Jews in Jerusalem, he told them, "This Jesus God has raised up, of which we are all witnesses" (Acts 2:31–32). That message was preached again and again and again (Acts 3:15; 4:10, 33). If the main message of the apostles is ethics (i.e., love, forgiveness, peace), they would have no reason to concoct a resurrection since that would be unnecessary to the message. But if the primary message was the resurrection of Jesus, the question remains why would they invent the resurrection and how could they have consistently lied about it for years? No plausible reason exists.

The Disciples Simply Lied

If Jesus did not rise physically, then the disciples lied by preaching that he did. What motivation could they possibly have for doing that? What could they gain? People might say that they needed the resurrection to start their new religion. But they were not "starting a religion." They *had* a religion—Judaism—and they had no intention of becoming anything else. The coming of the Messiah was the fulfillment of God's promise to the Jewish people. If Jesus did not rise as he said he would, he was a false prophet. His disciples would have been disappointed but they would have looked and waited for someone else to be the Messiah rather than create a lie about Jesus. There is no historical suggestion that the apostles lied about the resurrection. They were the eyewitnesses and always insisted upon the absolute truth and reality of Jesus' physical resurrection. On Friday they were fearful and in hiding, but after they experienced the Risen Lord, they had no fear. They bravely faced every danger insisting on the truth of their experience and their message. They went to their deaths cheerfully because they knew that death was not the end. While people are willing to die for what they believe is true, even if they are mistaken, no one would be motivated to die for a lie, certainly not hundreds of people. The apostles did not preach for a few days or weeks that Jesus rose but for the rest of their lives. They left everything they knew and loved to spread that *specific* message.

Today, the apostles are admired and respected, but during their lifetimes they suffered greatly for their message. Paul describes his life as an apostle, and no doubt it was typical: beatings and imprisonments by both Romans and Jews, being hungry and cold, the physical hardships of travelling, being ambushed by robbers, swimming across rivers, shipwrecks, braving heat and cold (2 Cor 11:21–27). In the end, nearly all of the apostles died by torture—not because they insisted that we should "love our neighbor" but because they insisted that Jesus Christ had risen from the dead. The conversion of St. Paul (Saul of Tarsus) also speaks to the truth of the resurrection. Saul/Paul passionately opposed the Jesus movement even arresting and imprisoning the followers of Jesus (Acts 8:3). But he too dramatically changed when he experienced the risen Christ himself (Acts 9:1–19). Did Saul, the man who devoted himself to snuffing out this Jesus movement, also lie? What would compel anyone, let alone hundreds of apostles, to endure such suffering and deprivation if in fact that essential message was a lie? It is inconceivable that hundreds of people would conspire to concoct such a lie and that every single one of them would maintain it for the rest of their lives when they had nothing to gain by it and everything to lose. No apostolic eyewitness ever recanted his or her claim that Jesus rose from the dead. If they had, that certainly would have been seized upon and mentioned by Roman or Jewish writers.

They Had Nothing Else to Live For, Nothing Else to Do

The apostles were all devout Jews. They loved their religion. They loved their homeland, their families, their work, their lives, just as much as we do. But they willingly relinquished everything after experiencing the resurrection. It is ludicrous to suggest that hundreds of people conspired to lie about the resurrection and were willing to endure tremendous hardships and even death by torture "just because" they really had nothing else going for them in their lives. It is unreasonable in the extreme to suggest that before the twenty-first century and the advent of technology people had no reason to live and their lives had no value or meaning. Something profoundly earthshaking happened to the followers of Jesus which caused them to leave everything they knew and loved to tell the world what they had experienced: The Messiah has come and he has risen from the dead.

People Were Simple-Minded and More Gullible Back Then

The hundreds of apostles who preached that Jesus rose did not have to be taught or convinced that he rose. Later generations would believe on the basis of the apostles' testimony, but they were the eyewitnesses. They did not have to be "convinced" of their experience, therefore it had nothing to do with their intelligence or naiveté. Either they experienced the resurrection or they did not. Furthermore, people were no less intelligent then. The ancients created amazing wonders, such as the Parthenon, the pyramids and the Colosseum, all without the calculators, computers, technology or the machinery which we have today. To accomplish these feats without modern advantages suggests that the ancients may have been *more* intelligent and capable than we are, not less so. People were not idiots simply because they lived long ago.

Mythology Inspired the Idea of the Resurrection

The idea that Christians simply copied pagan myths and invented stories about Jesus is currently popular especially on the internet. The earliest written account of the resurrection is found in Paul's First Epistle to the Corinthians (1 Cor 15). When Paul wrote that letter, many eyewitnesses of the resurrection were still alive. These witnesses would have not invented the idea of the resurrection and they had no motivation to create such a lie. But above all, they certainly would not have adopted ideas from pagan mythology since all of the early followers of Jesus were *Jews*, not former pagans who were "religion shopping." If they were to create something appealing for people to follow, they certainly would not have invented a crucified Messiah who was a poor Jewish rabbi! The first followers of Jesus (we cannot really call them "Christians" since that term did not exist) would have been repulsed by the very notion of "borrowing" from pagan mythology since Jews rejected everything about paganism. These first believers were simply Jews who believed that Jesus was the Messiah, the only difference between them and other Jews. "Christianity" did not exist.

Some people point to myths such as that of the Greek god Adonis or the Egyptian god Osiris as providing the inspiration for Christian claims about the resurrection. But when we take a look at these myths and compare them to the resurrection of Jesus, in fact they bear no similarity. Those mythologies consist of very different patterns and do not form a consistent motif of the dying and rising god,[2] certainly not in the way Jesus' resurrection is understood or described. The mythological gods who die and "return" in some form were generally believed to be brought back to life in the spring by a fertility or earth goddess.[3] Not surprisingly, these stories were associated with harvest. Jesus is not a harvest god. He was not said to return for a period of time and then disappear again, only to return the following year. The most important fact is that Jesus was a real, historical person. Countless eyewitnesses affirmed that they had seen him alive again after he died. No one ever claimed to have witnessed the rising of these mythological figures. In fact, the pagan gods typically did not "rise" from the dead. Rather they "returned" or were restored back to life for part of the year with the springtime vegetation.

2. Tryggve Mettinger, *Riddle of Resurrection: "Dying and Rising Gods" in the Ancient Near East* (Stockholm: Almqvist & Wiksell, 2001), 218. Cited by De Rose and Garry, "Death or Departure of the Gods," 17–23, 20.

3. Ibid.

PART 2—BASIC ISSUES THAT CONFRONT MOST CHRISTIANS

There Is No "Proof," and the Resurrection Does Not Conform to Science

The apostles experienced a profound event which transformed them forever. The resurrection is not easily dismissible. It cannot be *proven* according to the demands of science, but that does not necessarily mean it did not happen. We can and should look at other evidence, namely *the effect*. You see water on the ceiling. You do not have to see the leaking pipe or roof to know that you have a leak: you can see the effect. Every day we arrive at logical conclusions based on the effects of events, even if we did not witness the actual event. This is evidence. These are clues to what happened. From such clues and evidence we draw a logical inference.

It is perhaps because of the confidence derived from our cumulating scientific knowledge that we describe these patterns as inviolable "laws." However, true science—that is, science unmixed with certain metaphysical assumptions—can only tell us what *is* observed; not what *can* or *cannot* be observed. It can never rule out the possibility of a deviation from the patterns we observe. Science deals with that which can be observed, measured, quantified, tested and evaluated. Science deals with the natural world. God, as eternal and uncreated, stands outside of the natural order, outside of the universe. He is not part of it nor is he subject to it. God cannot be observed or tested by scientific methods. A miracle, such as the resurrection, is an exceptionally rare and religiously-meaningful deviation from what is generally observed in nature.

Through the scientific method, we have greatly enhanced our ability to detect and explain patterns in the natural world's operation. And yet much of it remains a mystery. Most of the universe consists of dark matter. It cannot be seen, yet scientists know that it is there because of how it affects the "normal" matter in the universe. The dominant force in the universe is "dark energy."[4] Scientists assumed that after the big bang the universe would be slowing down or might begin contracting. However, they were amazed to discover that the universe continues to expand. The force theorized responsible for the inexplicable and continuous expansion of the universe is known as "dark energy." It too cannot be seen, and yet scientists conclude that it exists because of its effects. Likewise even though the resurrection of Christ cannot be "explained" or "proven" its effects remain. The most important evidence is the existence of the church. Christianity would

---

4. NASA, "Dark Energy, Dark Matter."

not exist had the apostles not witnessed the resurrection and testified about that to countless people throughout the Roman Empire.

Although miracles cannot be "predicted" one miracle occurs every year with absolute regularity and it affirms the resurrection of Jesus Christ: the "Holy Fire."[5] This miracle is known to Orthodox Christians but surprisingly it is almost completely unknown in the West. On Great Saturday afternoon, the day before Pascha (Easter) on the Orthodox calendar, crowds pack the Church of the Holy Sepulcher (also known as the Church of the Resurrection) in anticipation of the Holy Fire. Flashes of blue light appear within the darkened church. The patriarch (bishop) of Jerusalem enters the tomb of Christ with an unlit candle and wearing a simple robe. The patriarch is searched and the tomb is thoroughly searched by Muslims or Israelis for any incendiary device. Finding none, the patriarch enters the tomb of Christ, shuts the door and prays in complete darkness inside the tomb until his candle is miraculously lit. This is the miracle of the Holy Fire. The patriarch distributes the flame to the waiting faithful outside the tomb who are also holding unlit candles, which also sometimes spontaneously alight even before the fire is passed to them. The Holy Fire is not ordinary fire but has a different color and quality. For the first few minutes it does not burn even when people insert their hands into the flame. This miracle, including blue flashing lights inside the church and spontaneously igniting candles, has been witnessed and attested to by pilgrims to Jerusalem since the early centuries of Christianity, long before the invention of electricity or matches.

The resurrection cannot be scientifically proven since God is not part of the created world, and thus is not subject to analysis by science. But the belief that something profound occurred which changed the world and the course of history forever is more logical than dismissing it by saying that "nothing happened." This would make the resurrection the most widespread and successful deception ever perpetrated. The truth is that the resurrection is a historical event which transformed the disciples of Jesus and became the foundation and purpose of the church. It is the reason why God became man: to destroy the power of death and grant eternal life. Christ is risen.

---

5. See http://www.holyfire.org/eng.

5

A Second Look at the God of the Old Testament

Fr. Lawrence Farley

IN THE EARLY SECOND century, a teacher was making a big splash in the church in Rome, and his name was Marcion. His main idea was that the God of the Old Testament was not the father of our Lord Jesus Christ. The deity of the Old Testament was utterly unlike the God of love proclaimed by Jesus—this Jewish God was fierce, vengeful, war-like, and maybe a little bit weird with his insistence on circumcision as the sign of his covenant. Accordingly, Marcion threw out the entirety of the Old Testament and took a scalpel to the New Testament, keeping only a few of St. Paul's letters (he liked Galatians) and a greatly abbreviated Gospel of St. Luke. Despite his donation of two hundred thousand sesterces to the local Roman church (quite a sum in those days), he was excommunicated and his money duly returned. No doubt Marcion would have agreed with Richard Dawkins in his assessment of this Old Testament deity as "the most unpleasant character in all fiction."

Why the vigorous reaction on the part of the local Roman clergy? The Roman church, like every other church in the world, had read the New Testament and knew that Jesus proclaimed that the Jewish God, the God of the Old Testament, was his Father. The Jewish temple in Jerusalem was his "Father's house" (see Luke 2:49 NIV), and Jesus was continually citing the Old Testament. There might be problems depending on how one interprets certain parts of the Old Testament, but throwing it out wholesale was not a solution which any Christian could accept.

Where, then, does the solution lie? A chapter of this size cannot deal with every objection which a detractor of Christianity might bring forth, but four things should be said.

First, Orthodox Christians do not view the Old Testament in the same way that Muslims view the Qur'an or that Orthodox Jews view their Torah. That is, we do not view the Old Testament as God's final and definitive word on the subjects with which it deals. For the Muslim, the Qur'an is indeed God's full, timeless, and final word. Presumably, Orthodox Jews have similar views regarding the Torah (the "Old Testament" in Christian terminology). Both Muslims and Orthodox Jews (as well as some fundamentalist Christians) regard sacred text as containing a full disclosure of the unchangeable divine will on the subjects on which it pronounces.

Orthodox Christians view the Old Testament differently—not as constituting God's final and unchangeable decree, but as the next step in his long striving to bring his people to Christ. In Paul's words, "Christ is the end [*telos* in the original Greek] of the law" (Rom 10:4); and "the Law was our tutor to bring us to Christ, that we might be justified by faith. But after faith has come, we are no longer under a tutor" (Gal 3:24–25). In other words, the Jewish law was never intended as God's final word and will for his people—Christ was the final word and will. The Law was intended as a step along the way to Christ, a tool to educate Israel as they learned the hard lessons of monotheism and righteousness and moved toward (sometimes "inched toward") Christ.

The Law was given to a people inclined to disobedience and idolatry. Even at the foot of Mount Sinai they renounced the covenant with God which they had just made, and worshipped the golden calf (Exod 32); and when they had crossed the Jordan a generation later, and were poised to possess the land, they still clung to their idols (Josh 24:19–24). They came from a culture where women were simply chattel and where all life was undervalued, a world where the rich bribed judges and ground the face of the poor, a world filled with gods, many of whom were arbitrary and dangerous. It was impossible for Israel to step from this culture and from these values into the world of the Sermon on the Mount in a single step or even within a single generation. Indeed, as it turned out, it would take many generations to drill into them the elementary notion that the gods of the nations around them were powerless idols and should not be worshipped. The Law was given to Israel to begin this long journey to the values of the Gospel and of Christ. According to Christ himself (see Matt 19:7–8), some of the provisions of the Law (such as those providing for divorce) were only given because the people had hard hearts, and could not immediately bear the full weight of God's final will. Here the Law was not God's final word, but a temporary provisional one, to be replaced with the Gospel word in the fullness of time. Much of the Old Testament legislation needs to be received in this light, as baby steps in a long and winding road to maturity.

Second, the Law was given to Israel not as a philosophical document for individuals, but as a constitution and charter for a people. God's covenant was not made with individual Jews, but with a nation. Israel was what some nations could only aspire to be—one nation truly under God—and that is why certain behaviours (such as idolatry) were not just sins but crimes, for renouncing God and breaking his covenant imperilled national existence. The various laws are misread if read apart from this context. It would be nonsensical, for example, for America to mandate such laws, for America is not a theocracy in covenant with God, whatever it may write on its coins. Israel, however, was under covenant with God, and therefore knew no separation between "church and state."

Furthermore, like most states today, it was forced to confront the moral dilemma of war-making. Any nation, then as now, must be willing to wage war if it is to survive. In its original historical context, the options for Israel as a nation were not "to fight or not to fight," but rather "to fight or to be annihilated." The world into which Israel was born was a terrible place (has it changed much?), and war was a part of it. We need to read the Law as marching orders to a nation which lived under constant threat from bigger, more powerful, and ruthless neighbors. The voice of the psalmist could be taken as the expression of their continual national dilemma: "I am for peace; but when I speak, they are for war" (Ps 120:7).

Third, Orthodox Christians read the Old Testament on two levels, looking both to the historical level of meaning and also to a deeper spiritual level. Medieval exegetes have described these levels as the literal, the allegorical, the moral, and the anagogical, and even produced a rhyming couplet to explain the differences (in English the Latin couplet reads: "the letter speaks of deeds; allegory to faith, the moral how to act, anagogy our destiny"). The principle of a deeper meaning goes back to St. Paul (and before him, to the Jewish rabbis): in Galatians 4:21ff., St. Paul examines the story of Sarah and Hagar as found in Genesis 16, and interprets the story in terms not only of two women and their sons, but two covenants, the Old and the New. Whether we call this "Jewish midrash" or regard it as allegory, or as typology, or simply as identifying and applying the basic principles undergirding the literal Old Testament text matters little. What does matter is that Paul finds a deeper meaning in the text, one that applies to Christ and his church, and Christians ever after him have followed in his exegetical footsteps (at least until the Reformation, when certain excesses of interpretation caused some Reformers to renege on the whole allegorical/ typological method).

This greatly influences how Christians read the Old Testament, and differentiates classical Christian interpretation from Jewish interpretation (as well as that of some modern Evangelical Christians). Take for example the graphic verses of Psalm 137, which speak of a blessing on the pagans who requite the Babylonians for the destruction of Jerusalem by destroying them in turn: "Happy the one who repays you as you have served us! Happy the one who takes and dashes Your little ones against the rock!" Its literal meaning is plain enough—it is a heart-rending cry of pain, saying to Babylon in effect, "What goes around comes around." But how can Christians piously pray this psalm? Not only has Babylon vanished from the earth, but we are told to love our enemies, not invoke God's wrath on them. Our true enemies are not flesh and blood people (see Eph 6:12), but demonic armies in the heavenlies. Paul's words here provide the answer: we do set our faces in fury against the foe, but our foes are not people, but demons and sins. This psalm calls us to exercise the same ruthless implacable hatred of our sins that the psalmist once showed to his Babylonian destroyers.

Or take another example, that of the city of Jerusalem. In the literal reading of the psalms, Jerusalem is just a city, occupying a few acres in southern Palestine. But a deeper reading of the text and a longer perusal of underlying pervasive principles reveal a deeper meaning: Jerusalem is an image of the Mother of God. For God dwells in Zion. After the exile, the prophets looked forward to his return to Zion, a return which would save his people. Thus the prophet Zechariah: "Sing and rejoice, O daughter of Zion! For behold, I am coming and I will dwell in your midst . . . Many nations shall be joined to the Lord in that day, and they shall become My people" (Zech 2:10–11). The Christian reads this and stops and rubs his eyes. What's this? Zion, a woman? Even a "virgin daughter"? (Isa 37:22). And God will come and dwell within her? It is impossible for a Christian not to see the incarnation in these verses, and regard the Virgin Daughter of Zion in whom God comes to dwell as prefiguring the Virgin Mother of God. God dwells in his temple in Zion, and she has become that temple.

The image contains a further richness, for Mary is both virgin and mother, just as the church is both virgin and mother (see 2 Cor 11:2–3; Gal 4:26). Mary and the church are thus both our mother, and it is significant, therefore, that the church, the woman clothed with the sun in Revelation 12, is also described as having given birth to Christ (v. 5). In the apocalyptic image, the church bears the face of Mary, so that in this way the various levels of meaning coalesce and combine. A classic Orthodox reading of the Old Testament yields richer results than a simple literal one.

Finally, to really appreciate the nature of the Law, we need to read it in its historical context as a late Bronze Age document, and not compare it with our modern democratic value system. If comparisons are to be made, one should compare the Law with the Code of Hammurabi (ca. 1770 BC), not Rousseau's *Social Contract*. As mentioned before, life in the late Bronze Age was short and brutal. Kings were valued, and the mass of men were considered spectacularly expendable, a kind of human ballast. In this cultural context, the Law shines with brilliance, and offers a view of human worth far ahead of its time.

Take, for example, the early creation stories. In the ancient world, only kings were regarded as bearing the divine image, but in the Genesis creation story, the common man bears the divine image—and that includes the common woman. In fact, she with her husband share jointly the rule and stewardship of the earth (Gen 1:26–28). Here woman is not chattel, but a co-ruler with her husband over all the earth. Kings are nowhere in sight; it is the commoner—of both genders—who is here exalted.

Or take the example of a law regulating warfare in Deuteronomy 20:19–20, which forbids harming the environment with a scorched earth policy: "When you besiege a city for a long time, while making war against it to take it, you shall not destroy its trees by wielding an ax against them; if you can eat of them, do not cut them down to use in the siege, for the tree of the field *is* man's *food*. Only the trees which you know *are* not trees for food you may destroy and cut down, to build siegeworks against the city that makes war with you, until it is subdued." Or take the example of a law demanding respect for the dignity of the poor, as found in Deuteronomy 24:10–11: "When you lend your brother anything, you shall not go into his house to get his pledge. You shall stand outside, and the man to whom you lend shall bring the pledge out to you." Or take the example of a law mandating free food to the poor, as found in Leviticus 19:9–10: "When you reap the harvest of your land, you shall not wholly reap the corners of your field, nor shall you gather the gleanings of your harvest. And you shall not glean your vineyard, nor shall you gather every grape of your vineyard; you shall leave them for the poor and the stranger." Or take the example of the law mandating care of one's poor neighbor, as found in Leviticus 25:35: "If one of your brethren becomes poor, and falls into poverty among you, then you shall help him, like a stranger or a sojourner, that he may live with you."

Or take the example of the laws governing slavery. Critics of Christianity have long slammed the Bible for accepting slavery, but seemingly few have troubled themselves to read up on what the Bible actually says about it. Slavery was a cultural fact in the ancient world, both in days of the Old Testament and the New (rather like usury is today). It is all the more significant that the Law limits slavery with provisions like the following:

> If you buy a Hebrew servant, he shall serve six years; and in the seventh he shall go out free and pay nothing. (Exod 21:2)

> If your brother, a Hebrew man, or a Hebrew woman, is sold to you and serves you six years, then in the seventh year you shall let him go free from you. And when you send him away free from you, you shall not let him go away empty-handed; you shall supply him liberally from your flock, from your threshing floor, and from your winepress. (Deut 15:12–14)

Here we see that slavery in Israel was meant to be a temporary remedy for poverty. It falls short of the ideal of no slavery at all, but these laws still constituted a tremendous advance over the culture of its day, and (need it be added?) over slavery as practiced in the American South generations ago.

These examples reveal that the Old Testament was not quite the seething, vengeful, unenlightened volume that many imagine it to be. The God who gave these laws was concerned for the environment, with the welfare, dignity, and pride of the poor. Slavery, universal throughout the world, was mitigated among his people, and could only last six years, and ended with the former slave being enriched as he left. These things were not just unusual for their time. In some ways they are in advance of parts of our culture even today. Perhaps the God to whom these laws are ascribed deserves a second look.

PART 3

The Church and Her Teaching

6

Bible Only? The Orthodox Teaching on Sola Scriptura

Fr. John Whiteford

DESPITE THE DIVERSITY OF doctrine and practice among Protestants, there is one doctrine that all affirm. It is *sola scriptura*; more than any other doctrine, this truly is the *sine qua non* of Protestantism. The Westminster Confession defines *sola scriptura* thusly:

> The supreme judge by which all controversies of religion are to be determined, and all decrees of councils, opinions of ancient writers, doctrines of men, and private spirits, are to be examined, and in whose sentence we are to rest, can be no other but the Holy Spirit speaking in the Scripture.[1]

The 39 Articles of Anglicanism, which have long been included in the Anglican *Book of Common Prayer*, say:

> Holy Scripture containeth all things necessary to salvation: so that whatsoever is not read therein, nor may be proved thereby, is not to be required of any man, that it should be believed as an article of the Faith, or be thought requisite or necessary to salvation. In the name of the Holy Scripture we do understand those canonical Books of the Old and New Testament, of whose authority was never any doubt in the Church.[2]

---

1. Schaff, *Creeds of Christendom*, 3:605.
2. Ibid., 489.

Part 3—The Church and Her Teaching

Such definitions could be multiplied, but they essentially affirm the same idea: only Scripture is an infallible guide on matters of faith and piety, and it alone is binding on the conscience.

The problem is that this is held to be an essential doctrine, but when we look to Scripture *alone* for evidence of this doctrine, we find nothing of the sort. Many verses can be cited which speak of the authority, importance, profitability, and infallibility of Scripture, but nowhere in Scripture do we find that Scripture *alone* is authoritative, important, profitable, infallible, or that it is *alone* binding on the conscience. In fact, in Scripture, we find quite the opposite. For example, 2 Thessalonians 2:15 says: "Therefore, brethren, stand fast and hold the traditions which you were taught, whether by word or our epistle." For one thing, this tells us that St. Paul's Epistles are themselves tradition, and so contradicts the usual dichotomy between Scripture and tradition that *sola scriptura* advocates espouse. Furthermore, this also puts apostolic oral tradition on the same level as Scripture.

Typically, proponents of *sola scriptura* cite all the negative statements in the Gospels about the traditions of the Pharisees, while ignoring (or even obfuscating)[3] the positive references to tradition elsewhere. However the Greek word for "tradition" is *paradosis*—which, though translated differently in some Protestant versions of the Bible, is the same word used when referring negatively to the false teachings of the Pharisees (Mark 7:3, 5, 8), and also when referring positively to authoritative Christian teaching (1 Cor 11:2; 2 Thess 2:15; 3:6). The word itself literally means "what is transmitted" or "what is passed on." So what makes the traditions of the Pharisees false and that of the church true? The source! Christ made clear what the source of the tradition of the Pharisees was, when he called it "the tradition of men" (Mark 7:8). St. Paul on the other hand, in reference to Christian tradition states, "Now I praise you, brethren, that you remember me in all things and keep the traditions [*paradoseis*] just as I delivered [*paredoka*, a verbal form of *paradosis*] them to you" (1 Cor 11:2). But where did he get these traditions in the first place? "I received from the Lord that which I delivered

---

3. "The NIV translators, however, have effected what amounts to a literary sleight of hand. One would be tempted to call it a rather nifty move were it not for the fact that they have tampered with the written Word of God. Hold the traditions which ye have been taught. Traditions (*paradoseis*) is a noun in the objective case. It is derived from the verb to hand over (*paradidomi*). The phrase, which ye have been taught (*edidachthate*), is a form of to teach (*didasko*). The NIV turns the verb into the noun—hold to the teachings—and turns the noun into the verb—we passed on to you. If we were to translate the NIV translation back into Greek, instead of *paradoseis*, we would have *didaskalias*, and instead of *edidachthate* we would have *paredothate*." Carlton, *The Way*, 137.

[*paredoka*] to you" (1 Cor 11:23). This is what the Orthodox Church refers to when it speaks of the apostolic tradition—"the faith which was once for all delivered [*paradotheise*] to the saints" (Jude 3). Its source is Christ, it was delivered personally by him to the apostles through all that he said and did, which if it were all written down, "the world itself could not contain the books that would be written" (John 21:25). The apostles delivered this knowledge to the entire church, and the church, being the repository of this treasure thus became "the pillar and ground of the truth" (1 Tim 3:15).

One other key weakness of the doctrine of *sola scriptura* is that, when pressed, those who advocate it have to admit that it could not have functioned during the time that the apostles were still living, because they acknowledge that the apostles themselves we no less authoritative when they passed on the teachings of Christ orally than they were when those teachings were later written down. And so somehow they have to argue that a doctrine that could not have functioned during the time the New Testament was written was nevertheless taught by the New Testament.

Furthermore, it must be acknowledged that the Bible did not come with an authoritative table of contents, and so one must concede that it was the church that decided what books would be in the Bible in the first place. However, to avoid acknowledging that the church has the authority to bind the conscience on this question, proponents of *sola scriptura* make the odd argument that "the Bible is a fallible collection of infallible books"[4]—in other words, in order to avoid acknowledging the authority of the church, they have to concede that there may be some books that should not be in the Bible that are, and that there may be some books that should be in the Bible that are not, but nevertheless argue that whatever books rightly should be in the Bible are infallible.

Did the Fathers Teach *Sola Scriptura*?

In recent years, defenders of this teaching have felt the sting of the argument that the doctrine of *sola scriptura* is not taught in Scripture, and so fails to meet its own criteria. Also, the past few decades has seen a steady stream of converts to either Orthodoxy or Roman Catholicism because the weakness of this foundational teaching has been exposed. Consequently, some apologists have attempted to turn the tables on Orthodox and Roman

---

4. Sproul, "Establishment of Scripture," 66.

Catholic apologists, and have tried to argue that *sola scriptura* is itself taught by tradition.[5]

In order to prove that the fathers taught *sola scriptura*, one would have to find them teaching not only that Scripture was of primary importance, authoritative, and binding on the conscience—but also that Scripture *alone* was an authority binding on the conscience.

There are a number of proof texts that are cited, but for the sake of brevity, let us look at three examples.

St. Irenaeus (AD 130–202)

> We have learned from none others the plan of our salvation, than from those through whom the gospel has come down to us, which they did at one time proclaim in public, and, at a later period, by the will of God, handed down to us in the Scriptures, to be the ground and pillar of our faith.[6]

Interestingly, St. Irenaeus is alluding here to 1 Timothy 3:15: "but if I am delayed, I write so that you may know how you ought to conduct yourself in the house of God, which is the church of the living God, the pillar and ground of the truth." The church is the pillar and ground of the truth. The Scriptures are the texts of the church.

It should be obvious, however, that nowhere does St. Ireneaus suggest that Scripture alone is the pillar and ground of our faith. The fact that he did not believe in *sola scriptura* is made very clear by other things he says in the same work. For example:

> As I said before, the Church, having received this preaching and this Faith, although she is disseminated throughout the whole world, yet guarded it, as if she occupied but one house. She likewise believed these things just as if she had but one soul and one and the same heart; and harmoniously she proclaims them and teaches them and hands them down, as if she possessed one mouth. For, while the languages of the world are diverse, nevertheless, the authority of the Tradition is one and the same. Neither do the Churches among the Germans believe otherwise or have another Tradition, nor do those among the Iberians, nor among the Celts, nor away in the East, or in Egypt, nor in Libya, nor those

---

5. White, "Sola Scriptura and the Early Church," 27–62.
6. Irenaeus, *Against Heresies*, 414.

which have been established in the central regions of the world. But just as the sun, that creature of God, is one and the same throughout the whole world, so also the preaching of the Truth shines everywhere and enlightens all men who desire to come to a knowledge of the Truth. Nor will any of the rulers in the Churches, whatever his power of eloquence, teach otherwise, for no one is above the Teacher; nor will he who is weak in speaking subtract from the Tradition. For the Faith is one and the same, and cannot be amplified by one who is able to say much about it, nor can it be diminished by one who can say but little.[7]

When, therefore, we have such proofs, it is not necessary to seek among others the Truth which is easily obtained from the Church. For the Apostles, like a rich man in a bank, deposited with her most copiously everything which pertains to the Truth, and everyone whosoever wishes draws from her the drink of life. For she is the entrance to life, while all the rest are thieves and robbers. That is why it is surely necessary to avoid them, while cherishing with the utmost diligence the things pertaining to the Church, and to lay hold of the Traditions of Truth. What then? If there should be a dispute over some kind of question, ought we not have recourse to the most ancient Churches in which the Apostles were familiar, and draw from them what is clear and certain in regard to that question? What if the Apostles had not in fact left writings to us? Would it not be necessary to follow the order of Tradition, which was handed down to those whom they entrusted the Churches?[8]

Many of the heretical groups that St. Irenaeus responded to also claimed to follow the Scriptures. And though St. Irenaeus refuted them with Scripture, he also refuted them by appealing to the tradition of the church, which is where the correct understanding of Scripture is to be found.

St. Basil (AD 330–379)

Those hearers who are instructed in the Scriptures should examine what is said by the teachers, receiving what is in conformity with the Scriptures and rejecting what is opposed to them.[9]

---

7. Ibid., 331.
8. Ibid., 416.
9. Basil, *Ascetical Works*, 185.

Part 3—The Church and Her Teaching

This quote from St. Basil, taken in isolation, sounds like it might support the position of those adhering to *sola scriptura*, but there are two problems with this interpretation: first, it assumes that St. Basil would have interpreted the Scriptures apart from tradition, or that at least if he did, he would not have considered tradition to be binding on his conscience while interpreting Scripture—which is not at all stated here. But we do not have to guess at this. St. Basil left us with more than enough of his writings for us to determine what authority he gave to tradition. In his treatise on the Holy Spirit, he argues that the Holy Spirit is a person, and cites the doxology ("Glory to the Father, and to the Son, and to the Holy Spirit") in support of that argument. He counters the objection that the doxology, though an ancient part of the universal liturgical tradition of the church, is not found in Scripture by saying:

> Of the beliefs and practices whether generally accepted or publicly enjoined which are preserved in the Church some we possess derived from written teaching; others we have received delivered to us "in a mystery" by the tradition of the apostles; and both of these in relation to true religion have the same force. And these no one will gainsay;—no one, at all events, who is even moderately versed in the institutions of the Church. For were we to attempt to reject such customs as have no written authority, on the ground that the importance they possess is small, we should unintentionally injure the Gospel in its very vitals; or, rather, should make our public definition a mere phrase and nothing more. For instance, to take the first and most general example, who is thence who has taught us in writing to sign with the sign of the cross those who have trusted in the name of our Lord Jesus Christ? What writing has taught us to turn to the East at the prayer? Which of the saints has left us in writing the words of the invocation at the displaying of the bread of the Eucharist and the cup of blessing? For we are not, as is well known, content with what the apostle or the Gospel has recorded, but both in preface and conclusion we add other words as being of great importance to the validity of the ministry, and these we derive from unwritten teaching. Moreover we bless the water of baptism and the oil of the chrism, and besides this the catechumen who is being baptized. On what written authority do we do this? Is not our authority silent and mystical tradition? Nay, by what written word is the anointing of oil itself taught? And whence comes

the custom of baptizing thrice [i.e., by triple immersion]? And as to the other customs of baptism from what Scripture do we derive the renunciation of Satan and his angels? Does not this come from that unpublished and secret teaching which our fathers guarded in a silence out of the reach of curious meddling and inquisitive investigation? Well had they learnt the lesson that the awful dignity of the mysteries is best preserved by silence. What the uninitiated are not even allowed: to look at was hardly likely to be publicly paraded about in written documents. What was the meaning of the mighty Moses in not making all the parts of the tabernacle open to every one? The profane he stationed without the sacred barriers; the first courts he conceded to the purer; the Levites alone he judged worthy of being servants of the Deity; sacrifices and burnt offerings and the rest of the priestly functions he allotted to the priests; one chosen out of all he admitted to the shrine, and even this one not always but on only one day in the year, and of this one day a time was fixed for his entry so that he might gaze on the Holy of Holies amazed at the strangeness and novelty of the sight.[10]

St. Basil is not trying to convince anyone that Christians should be baptized by a triple immersion—he is appealing to the fact that everyone at that time accepted this unwritten tradition in order to argue for the authority of another extra-biblical tradition: the doxology, which in turn supports the teaching that the Holy Spirit is equal to the Father and the Son. And one has to ask, how did this universally accepted Christian tradition come to be universally accepted, if it did not come from the apostles themselves? However, the bottom line here is the question of the authority of the church. If you accept that the Orthodox Church is what it claims to be—the one, holy, catholic, and apostolic church established by Christ—then questions like this are easily answered.

St. John Chrysostom (AD 347–407)

Scripture, though, whenever it wants to teach us something like this, gives its own interpretation, and doesn't let the listener go astray . . . So, I beg you, block your ears against all distractions of that kind, and let us follow the norm of Sacred Scripture.[11]

---

10. Basil, *De Spiritu Sancto*, 40–42.
11. Chrysostom, *Homilies on Genesis 1–17*, 175.

In context, St. John Chrysostom was simply admonishing his hearers to interpret Scripture within the context of the rest of Scripture. Nowhere does he suggest that *only* Scripture is binding on the conscience, and in fact when commenting on 2 Thessalonians 2:15, he says:

> "Therefore brethren, stand fast and hold the traditions which you have been taught, whether by word or by our letter." From this it is clear that they did not hand down everything by letter, but there was much also that was not written. Like that which was written, the unwritten too is worthy of belief. Let us regard the Tradition of the Church also as worthy of belief. Is it Tradition? Seek no further.[12]

We could go on and on, but in every case, attempts to prove that the fathers taught *sola scriptura* fall flat.[13]

Solo Scriptura?

You may remember the scene in the classic film *Star Wars*, in which Obi-Wan Kenobi used a "Jedi mind-trick" on some Imperial storm troopers, and said: "These are not the droids you're looking for"—despite the fact that the droids in question really were the droids that they were looking for. One response to critiques of the doctrine of *sola scriptura* is essentially to argue: "This is not the doctrine of *sola scriptura* you're arguing against." They argue that it is only the version of *sola scriptura* of *some* believers that we have critiqued—a version they call "*solo scriptura*."[14] The basic argument is that while some, less refined, supporters of this doctrine might argue for Scripture alone—completely apart from any acknowledgment of tradition—other, more sophisticated adherents do make use of tradition, and so therefore, the arguments against *sola scriptura* that we make do not apply to them. But this is really just a rhetorical trick, with no more basis in truth than that of Obi-Wan Kenobi.

We readily acknowledge that many proponents of *sola scriptura* have a very strong concept of tradition, at least in theory. But the only time you hear mention of tradition in practice is when it comes to doctrines like the doctrine of the Trinity, or Christology, or to some other historic doctrine

---

12. Chrysostom, *Homilies on Thessalonians*, 390.
13. For more on this, see Whiteford, *Responses to Protestant Apologists*.
14. Mathison, *Shape of Sola Scriptura*, 237–53.

that these apologists already agree with. However, if one took the tradition of the church seriously, he would practice praying for the dead, just to cite one example. This is a practice for which there is a massive amount of evidence in the early writings of the church. It was universally practiced, and there is no hint that it was ever controversial among Christians until the time of the Reformation.[15] You also find it referenced in the deuterocanonical books of the Old Testament (2 Macc 12:38–45 and Sir 7:33), and in 2 Timothy 1:16–18, St. Paul is praying for Onesiphorus, who obviously is no longer among the living:

> The Lord grant mercy to the household of Onesiphorus, for he often refreshed me, and was not ashamed of my chain; but when he arrived in Rome, he sought me out very zealously and found me. The Lord grant to him that he may find mercy from the Lord in that Day—and you know very well how many ways he ministered to me at Ephesus.

So clearly, even the more "sophisticated" apologists use tradition selectively. When it suits their purposes, St. Athanasius, St. John Chrysostom, and St. Augustine are let out of their cages, and allowed to speak in defense of historical Christian teachings, but when it does not suit them, those saints are told to get back into their cages, because their services are no longer required.

The response these apologists would make at this point is to say that they accept the core parts of the tradition that teach the fundamental truths found in the Creed, but when tradition is contradicted by Scripture, they will take Scripture over tradition because Scripture alone is binding on the conscience. But the problem here is not that Scripture *itself* contradicts tradition, but rather that their interpretation of Scripture contradicts the Orthodox tradition's interpretation. So then the question is not really whether we prefer Scripture over tradition—the real question is which tradition will we use to interpret the Bible? Which tradition can be trusted—the apostolic tradition, or these muddled, modern traditions that have no roots beyond the advent of the Reformation?

Another question that such apologists should ask themselves is why they should trust church tradition on the Creed, if they cannot trust it in general? Why should they, with a straight face, be able to appeal to historic Christian theology on the Trinity when they chide Jehovah's Witnesses for rejecting such theology, based on their reading of Scripture, when those

---

15. It should be noted that both Jews and Muslims also pray for the dead.

same apologists reject the historic Christian understanding of that part of the Creed that speaks of "one, holy, catholic, and apostolic church"?

How Do You Know What Tradition Is Right?

One other major counterargument that is made in defense of *sola scriptura*, is that we cannot know what tradition we should follow, since long before the Reformation, there were schisms; and even within the Orthodox Catholic tradition, you find fathers who did not agree. While it is true that there are schisms that have persisted to this day (Nestorians, Monophysites [or Non-Chalcedonians], and Roman Catholics), it cannot be denied that the Faith of the Nicene Creed is that there is only one church, that is one in doctrine and communion—not just some fuzzy, pluralistic invisible "church" that cannot agree doctrinally. The councils that canonized the Creed (as well as the Scriptures) also anathematized those who were outside the church, whether they were heretics, such as the Montanists, or schismatics like the Donatists. They did not say, "Well, we cannot agree with the Montanists doctrinally but they are just as much a part of the church as we are." Rather heretics and schismatics were excluded from the communion of the church until they returned, and were united with her. To even join in prayer with those outside the church was, and still is, forbidden (Canons of the Holy Apostles, canons XLV, XLVI). Unlike those who make heroes of those who break away from another group and start their own, in the early church this was considered among the most damnable sins. As St. Ignatius of Antioch (a disciple of the apostle John) warned in his epistle to the Philadelphians, "Do not be misled, my brothers: if anyone follows a schismatic, he will not inherit the kingdom of God."[16]

So one has to conclude that either the Creed is wrong on this point, and that no such unified church exists, or they have to look at those bodies that have a plausible claim to being that church, and decide which one it is. But it should also be pointed out that the issues that separated the Orthodox from the Monophysites (or Non-Chalcedonians) and the Nestorians are on subtle issues that most Protestants would not think worth arguing over—but in most other respects, even though we have been divided from these groups for more than a thousand years, our theology and practice is

---

16. Lightfoot and Harmer, *Apostolic Fathers*, 107.

hardly distinguishable. This is an issue that is well beyond the scope of this essay, but on the issues upon which we do disagree, it is safe to say that most Protestant and Orthodox theologians are in agreement.

Our faith in the unity of the church has two aspects: it is both an historic and present unity. That is to say that when the apostles, for example, departed this life they did not depart from the unity of the church. They are as much a part of the church now as when they were present in the flesh. When we celebrate the eucharist in any local church, we do not celebrate it alone, but with the entire church, both on earth and in heaven. The saints in heaven are even closer to us than those we can see or touch. Thus, in the Orthodox Church we are not only taught by our contemporaries whom God has appointed to teach us, but by all those teachers of the church in heaven. We are as much and even more so under the teaching authority of Saint John Chrysostom today, as we are of our own bishop. The way this impacts our approach to Scripture is that we do not interpret it privately (2 Pet 1:20), but as a body. This approach to Scripture was given its classic definition by St. Vincent of Lérins:

> Here, perhaps, someone may ask: Since the canon of the Scripture is complete and more than sufficient in itself, why is it necessary to add to it the authority of ecclesiastical interpretation? As a matter of fact, [we must answer,] Holy Scripture, because of its depth, is not universally accepted in one and the same sense. The same text is interpreted differently by different people, so that one may almost gain the impression that it can yield as many different meanings as there are men . . . Thus it is because of the great many distortions caused by various errors, that it is, indeed, necessary that the trend of the interpretation of the prophetic and apostolic writings be directed in accordance with the rule of the ecclesiastical and Catholic meaning. In the Catholic Church itself, every care should be taken to hold fast to what has been believed everywhere, always, and by all. This is truly and properly Catholic, as indicated by the force and etymology of the name itself, which comprises everything truly universal. This general rule will be truly applied if we follow the principles of universality, antiquity, and consent. We do so in regard to universality if we confess that faith alone to be true which the entire Church confesses all over the world. [We do so] in regard to antiquity if we in no way deviate from those interpretations which our ancestors and fathers have manifestly proclaimed as inviolable. [We do so] in regard to consent if, in this

very antiquity, we adopt the definitions and propositions of all, or almost all, of the Bishops.[17]

So while it is true that individual fathers may at times disagree, it is in the patristic and conciliar consensus of the church that we find the doctrine of the one, holy, catholic and apostolic church that rightly guides our understanding of Scripture, and also preserves the oral apostolic tradition that Scripture tells us to keep (2 Thess 2:15).

---

17. Vincent of Lérins, *Fathers of the Church*, 7:269–71.

7

On Biblical Literalism

Gayle Woloschak

INTERPRETATION OF BIBLICAL TEXTS became an important part of Christian theology from the earliest days of the church, when the Bible was no more than the Old Testament. Many of the early church fathers (St. John Chrysostom, St. Augustine of Hippo, and many others) taught and wrote about the meaning of different biblical texts. Those interpretations were based on a variety of different methods, such as the consideration of a text's historical and cultural contexts. Reference to patristic writings on biblical interpretation continues to be an important aspect of the Orthodox approach to Scripture. Fr. George Florovsky put this historical aspect into context by writing:

> The Bible is intrinsically historical . . . [in it] we hear not only the voice of God but also the voice of man . . . Herein lies the miracle and mystery of the Bible, that it is the Word of God in human idiom.[1]

In light of the theological tradition of taking into consideration the church fathers, the iconography, the hymns, and so on, for biblical interpretation, what, then, is biblical literalism? Different authors have used different definitions of the term to explain different interpretive approaches to the Bible. The most common meaning is, as the phrase implies, an approach to understanding of biblical text by taking the words at face value exclusively and considering only the literal meaning of the text. In this case, the meaning of the text does not involve the use of metaphor or figurative language, but instead is based on the common definitions of the words

1. Florovsky, *Collected Works, Bible, Church, Tradition.*

used. Many contemporary Christians consider themselves to be biblical literalists, understanding the words of the text understood in a literal way. In addition, some biblical literalists contend that the Bible has no mistakes in it; that the text itself is inerrant.

Throughout the teachings of the early church fathers, we can find numerous warnings about the danger of reading Scripture while interpreting the text literally. St. Maximus the Confessor noted:

> A person who seeks God with true devotion should not be dominated by the literal text, lest he unwittingly receives not God but things appertaining to God; that is, lest he feel a dangerous affection for the words of Scripture instead of for the Logos.[2]

The danger that St. Maximus is talking about is a possibility that the Scripture itself becomes more important than the Gospel message as a whole.

What, then, is an appropriate understanding of Scripture in the life of the Orthodox Church? The Orthodox interpretation of Scripture is based on the historical experience of the church, reflected not only in the scriptural text itself, but also in the liturgical life of the church, the hymnography and iconography (which often seek to interpret Scripture), commentaries from the church fathers, the sacramental (or mystical) theology of the church, the lives of the saints, statements of the councils, and more. In essence, Scripture is interpreted in all aspects of the wisdom of the church, expressed throughout its entire history and life. As Fr. Stylianopoulis, a noted theologian who has written several texts on biblical interpretation, explains:

> Orthodox theology holds to a person and dynamic, rather than mechanistic and verbal, concept of inspiration. God did not merely dictate words of propositions to passive authors, but rather he impacted personally their whole beings, allowing them actively to comprehend, interpret, and convey his will to others according to the limitations of their understanding and language.[3]

Based on this broad, yet deep, understanding of scriptural interpretation, as one attempts to fathom the meaning of a particular story or passage of the Bible, one must consider a number of questions—What did the church fathers write? What hymns were written and are sung about that

---

2. Maximus the Confessor, "Two Hundred Texts," 155.
3. Stylianopoulos, *New Testament*.

text? What feasts are associated with it? What icons are associated with that text? What are their messages? All of these questions need to be addressed in order comprehend a biblical text. This is far from a simple reading of a Bible passage and attempting to interpret on one's own what the text means, and it is equally far from treating the passage as if it were a mathematical formula. It is important to understand that a comprehensive investigation of the meaning of a biblical text gives us the wisdom and humility necessary for true faith, while it takes us away from a literal interpretation and moves us into a more whole and contextual understanding of the text.

One other important issue associated with biblical interpretation is the fact that the Bible was written in different languages (Hebrew and Greek), in a different time, and in a different culture. It is important to discern what the text meant to those for whom it was originally written, in the context of the vernacular and the cultural underpinnings of the times. Ignoring these issues leads to a total misunderstanding of the text.

Probably the greatest confusion resulting from biblical literalism in today's culture revolves around the issue of evolution. Biblical literalists claim that the texts of Genesis 1 or 2 are in direct opposition to biological evolution. While this chapter is not meant to be a defense of evolution,[4] this is a good example of the type of problems created by literalism. Broadly understood, the message of the Genesis text concerns who humans are in relation to God, why they commit evil deeds, and how humans can form an appropriate relationship with God. This message does not contradict current evolutionary theory, even if the literal meaning of the text can be seen as doing so. Moreover, a literal version of the Genesis story is contradictory to other creation stories in the Bible, including those in Job, Psalms, and other Wisdom texts, while the messages of these texts remain the same.

Closely tied with literal (mis)interpretation of Genesis is the charge to humanity to have dominion over the creatures of the world. The word "dominion" could be interpreted as a call for humanity to conquer the world and all its creatures. This view is not consistent with a deeper understanding of the passage, and it has lead to environmental exploitation and use of the Bible to justify inappropriate environmental practices. One can point to many other examples of how biblical literalism has led to misunderstandings about current issues.

---

4. For a work that does defend evolution, please see Woloschak, "Compatibility of the Principles of Evolution with Eastern Orthodoxy," 209–31.

Part 3—The Church and Her Teaching

The use of literal interpretations of the Bible is inconsistent with Orthodox approaches that seek to understand a biblical text based on a deeper study, taking into consideration how the church has historically interpreted that text and expressed that interpretation in hymnography, iconography, explanations in patristic texts, and more. The voice of the Orthodox (who by definition cannot be literalists) in current discussions on such issues as the environment and evolution ought to be heard. The current cacophony of "biblical" opinions in our social milieu needs to be questioned, and Orthodoxy offers a voice consistent with the ancient teachings of the church.

8

Free from the Law? On the Rules of Orthodoxy and Their Purpose

Mother Melania

When you think of the word "law," what other words spring to mind? "Judge"? "Punishment"? "Crime"? If you have particularly good experiences, perhaps it is "safety" or "security." It is a very safe bet, though, that one word that did *not* occur to you is "love."

Yet, for a Christian, that ought to be the first word that comes to mind. Why? Because Christ, when asked what the greatest commandment of the Law was, replied thus:

> "You shall love the Lord your God with all your heart, with all your soul, and with all your mind." This is the first and great commandment. And the second is like it: "You shall love your neighbor as yourself." On these two commandments hang all the Law and the Prophets. (Matt 22:37–40)

Any person of good will recognizes that being "free" from love of our neighbor is not freedom, but miserable slavery to our own selfish whims. Likewise, if the Christian claim is true—if God loves us so much that Jesus Christ, the Second Person of the Trinity, freely died so that we might be partakers of the divine nature (cf. 2 Pet 1:4)—then, clearly, to refuse to love God with every inch of our being is to reveal a profound lack of gratitude.

So, when the council of the apostles decided that Gentile Christians were not obliged to keep the Law (cf. Acts 15:1–29), and when St. Paul spoke of freedom from the Law (Rom 7:6), they certainly did not mean that Christians are free from love of God and neighbor—the very core of the Law. What, then, did they mean?

Part 3—The Church and Her Teaching

First, it is important to notice the word "the" in "the Law."[1] When the apostles decreed that the Gentiles were not obliged to keep the Law (cf. Acts 15:24), and when St. Paul took issue with those who insisted on following the Law, they were referring to the Old Testament Law, specifically the ritual aspects.[2] Neither St. Paul nor any other scripture writer would consider it a good thing to be free from law altogether. For example, we are told to obey those who rule over us in the church (Heb 13:17), as well as the civil authorities (Rom 13:1).

At times, moreover, when St. Paul rails against Christians who are clinging to *the* Law, he goes on to speak of a Law that they *should* follow. Thus, after the Romans 7 passage cited above, St. Paul goes on to say, "For *the law of the Spirit of life in Christ Jesus* has made me free from the law of sin and death" (Rom 8:2; 4, emphasis added). Similarly, after several chapters in which he chastises the Galatians for attempting to be justified through the Law (specifically by circumcision), St. Paul says, "Bear one another's burdens, and so fulfill *the law of Christ*" (Gal 6:2, emphasis added).

So, freedom from *the* Law does not mean that we are free from law altogether, but that we are free to obey a greater Law that leads to life in Christ, and to the ability to love each other.[3] Thus, "For Christ is the end

---

1. Interestingly, νόμος (law) is one of a small group of Greek nouns that do not necessarily employ the article. "Certain nouns referring to persons or things that, instead of being only one of a class, are unique are treated as proper nouns, the article being either inserted or omitted." Machen, *New Testament Greek for Beginners* (2nd ed.), 188.

2. Stylianopoulos writes the following concerning Gal 2:16-20:

> The key to this passage is to see that St. Paul is referring not to ethical works but to "works of the Law" (*erga tou nomou*), namely, the Mosaic Law.
>
> What are the works of the Mosaic Law? Anyone who studies Galatians carefully will note the apostle is referring to the Jewish religious practices of circumcision, dietary laws, and festivals (Gal 2:2–5, 12; 4:9; 5:1–6, 12; 6:12–15). The same reference to "works of the Law" is also primary in the Letter to the Romans (Rom 3:19–20, 27–30).

Stylianopoulos, *How Are We Saved?*

3. St. Augustine beautifully contrasts the giving of "the law of works" on Mt. Sinai with the giving of "the law of faith and the Spirit" at Pentecost:

> *There* the law was given outwardly, so that the unrighteous might be terrified (Ex 19:12, 16); *here* it was given inwardly, so that they might be justified. For this, "Thou shalt not commit adultery, Thou shalt not kill, Thou shalt not covet; and if there be any other commandment"—such, of course, as was written on those tables—"it is briefly comprehended," says he, "in this saying, namely, Thou shalt love thy neighbor as thyself.

of the law for righteousness to everyone who believes" (Rom 10:4). Those who are living in Christ have no need for *the* Law, not because they are lawless (cf. 1 Tim 1:5–9), but because they have the law of God written in their hearts (cf. Jer 31:33). For this reason, St. Paul could say, "All things are lawful for me, but all things are not helpful. All things are lawful for me, but I will not be brought under the power of any" (1 Cor 6:12). The law of God in his heart kept him from abusing his freedom by sinning against God or his brother.

Most modern Christians can easily agree with the above paragraph, but many have gotten the idea that the law of Christ is a very lenient one. On the contrary, the law of Christ is *stricter* than the Old Testament law.[4] Christ himself makes this clear in the Sermon on the Mount (e.g., see Matt 5:21–48). For example, he says,

> You have heard that it was said to those of old, "You shall not commit adultery." But I say to you that whoever looks at a woman to lust for her has already committed adultery with her in his heart. (Matt 5:27–28)

The reason for the stricter law is that the law of God is now written on the hearts of baptized believers because Christ and his Holy Spirit now indwell them, giving us great help.[5] Thus, we must observe the Law in our very hearts and not just in our external behavior.

> Love works no ill to his neighbor: therefore love is the fulfilling of the law" (Rom 13:9–10). Now this was not written on the tables of stone but "is shed abroad in our hearts by the Holy Spirit, who is given to us" (Rom 5:5). God's law, therefore, is love. "To it the carnal mind is not subject, neither indeed can be";(Rom 8:7) but when the works of love are written on tables to alarm the carnal mind, there arises the law of works and "the letter which kills" the transgressor; but when love itself is shed abroad in the hearts of believers, then we have the law of faith and the Spirit which gives life to one who loves.

Augustine, *Treatise on the Spirit and the Letter*, 340.

4. "For the bonds of the Law [νόμου] are broken . . . not that our standard may be lowered, but that it may be exalted." Chrysostom, *Commentary on Galatians*, 79.

5. St. John Chrysostom, commenting on Rom 8:2 ("For the law of the Spirit of life in Christ Jesus has made me free"), says the following:

> It is the Spirit he is here calling the law of the Spirit . . . And yet he named that of Moses as such, where he says, "For we know that the Law is spiritual." . . . Now what is the distinction between this and that? The other was merely given by the Spirit, but this even furnisheth those that receive it with the Spirit in large measure. Wherefore also he called it the law of life

We can all understand this from our own experience. When our parents insisted that we say "please" and "thank you" when we were small children, it was not with the expectation that we would be free from such rules as adults, but with the hope that we would have so deeply internalized these rules that we would have courteous and kind hearts.

Likewise, when God gave the Israelites the Old Testament Law as a tutor, it was not with the intention of freeing mankind from all law in our "adulthood," but of preparing us for the time when the Spirit of adoption would come into our hearts to make us true sons and heirs of God (cf. Gal 4:1–7).

Still, just as those who were well-trained as children do not necessarily grow up to be courteous, loving adults, those who have Christ's Spirit in their hearts do not always live in a manner that reflects his presence. Though we have the law of the spirit of life in our hearts, we often write spiritual graffiti over it to the point that the original writing is obscured.[6]

> in contradistinction to that of sin, not that of Moses. For when he says, It freed me from the law of sin and death, it is not the law of Moses that he is here speaking of, since in no case does he style it the law of sin . . . but it is that which warreth against the law of the mind. For this grievous war did the grace of the Spirit put a stop to, by slaying sin, and making the contest light to us and crowning us at the outstart, and then drawing us to the struggle with abundant help.

Chrysostom, *Homilies on Paul's Epistle to the Romans*, 773.

6. St. John Chrysostom starts his first homily on the Gospel according to St. Matthew as follows:

> It were indeed meet for us not at all to require the aid of the written Word, but to exhibit a life so pure, that the grace of the Spirit should be instead of books to our souls . . . But, since we have utterly put away from us this grace, come, let us at any rate embrace the second best course. For that the former was better, God hath made manifest . . . And Paul too, pointing out the same superiority, said, that they had received a law [νόμον] "not in tables of stone, but in fleshy tables of the heart . . .
>
> Reflect then how great an evil it is for us, who ought to live so purely as not even to need written words, but to yield up our hearts, as books, to the Spirit; now that we have lost that honor, and are come to have need of these, to fail again in duly employing even this second remedy.

Thus, to the Christian, Law in its highest sense is synonymous (or at least inseparably bound) with the grace of the Spirit in the heart. Scripture is a corrective law and medical remedy for the impure of heart. Chrysostom, *Homilies on the Gospel of St. Matthew*, 16–17.

Melania—On the Rules of Orthodoxy and Their Purpose

When that happens, we need external reminders and sometimes consequences to encourage us to clean off all the graffiti. Thus, the Orthodox Church from its very beginning has had its Canons, its "rules to live by,"[7] which both delineate the behaviors of those who are in fact living like true children of God[8] and provide consequences for those who are not. The point of these consequences is always restoration of our likeness to God. To change the analogy, the canons of the church are both descriptions of spiritual health and remedies for spiritual disease. A very famous canon makes this explicit:

> It behooves those who have received from God the power to loose and bind, to consider the quality of the sin and the readiness of the sinner for conversion, and to apply medicine suitable for the disease, lest if he is injudicious in each of these respects he should fail in regard to the healing of the sick man . . . that he may neither cast them down into the precipices of despair, nor loosen the bridle towards dissolution or contempt of life; but in some way or other, either by means of sternness and astringency, or by greater softness and mild medicines, to resist this sickness and exert himself for the healing of the ulcer.[9]

Now, you may be saying, "Okay, I can agree with you when it comes to clear moral questions, but what about all those other Orthodox rules, such as fasting and prostrations? Why do we need *them*?"

Perhaps the best way to answer that question is to tell a short anecdote. A certain bishop, when asked to talk about Orthodox spirituality, often starts by saying, "Orthodox spirituality is physical." When his listeners look puzzled, he goes on to talk of how, when he was a little boy going to serve in the altar for the first time, his priest gently but firmly pressed him down to make a prostration when going through the door.

What the little boy, later to be a bishop, learned was that we cannot separate our spiritual acts from the physical. If we think we can prostrate

---

7. Patsavos, *Canonical Tradition of the Orthodox Church*.

8. Brevity does not permit a discussion of canon law, but it is worth noting that many canons that are "on the books" have been changed or have fallen into disuse. Of course, this has sometimes been due to laxity, but when done properly, it is in recognition of the fact that the church exists in, and must speak to, real cultures and the people who live in these cultures. Thus, an excellent rule in one context may be a straitjacket in another. The Patsavos article cited directly above, which is worth reading in its entirety, addresses this issue well.

9. *Canons of the Council in Trullo*, 797.

the knees of our hearts when we have never learned to prostrate the knees of our bodies, we are fooling ourselves. If we do not discipline our bodies, which is relatively easy, how will we find the strength and courage to discipline our souls?

Another important reason that it is necessary to discipline ourselves is that we are not and never can be autonomous beings. We are members of a body, specifically the body of Christ (cf. 1 Cor 12:12–27). The liver cannot say, "What I do to myself has no effect on the rest of you!" A fatty liver is a detriment to the whole body. Likewise, if I gorge myself on food, that does not affect only me. It deprives the needy of money, food, and my attention, which I should have turned to them instead of to my own palate and stomach. Plus, the more "me-centered" I am, the less effectively I can play my part in the body.

To summarize, then, "law" or "the rules" is all about loving God and our neighbor. Sometimes, this is very obvious (e.g. thou shalt worship the Lord thy God and him alone; do not murder; do not steal). Other times, these rules have more to do with making us the kind of people who *can* truly love God and neighbor. If we embrace these rules, we will indeed find true freedom and the peace that passes all understanding.

9

Respect for Women and the Tradition of the Male Priesthood

Sister Margarete Roeber

IN A SOCIETY THAT actively encourages girls to break down all barriers, the Orthodox tradition of a male priesthood seems emblematic of everything modern women continue to strive against. Why would a well-educated, independent, and self-respecting woman give a second thought to a faith that debars her from its highest levels of leadership simply because of her gender? Indeed, for many women inquiring into Orthodoxy, the male priesthood remains a source of confusion and resentment. But asking whether the Orthodox Church views women as inferior to men is not the same as asking whether or not women can be ordained as Orthodox priests and bishops. Examining the two questions together can clarify how they address connected yet distinct issues. On the one hand, we have the nature of men and women, and on the other, the nature of the priesthood. Both matters are complex enough that Orthodox theologians continue to explore their depths. That the church has both simple statements of faith and practice, as well as complex conversations surrounding them, reveals a healthy engagement of the Orthodox Church with society, even while she professes the same faith in every generation.

Orthodox theologians are very clear on the value of women relative to men. At the heart of Orthodox anthropology is the belief that the human person is made in the image of God (Gen 1:26). This is what sets humanity apart as the crown of visible creation and provides the potential for each person to become ever more like God, in the process of *theosis*.[1] Orthodox

---

1. Lossky describes deification as the union of creatures with God and their

theologians, ancient and modern, affirm that the image of God is present in every woman, just as in every man.[2]

It is also critical to remember that the greatest of the saints in the Orthodox Church is the Virgin Mary, the *Theotokos* (literally, God-bearer). She is not considered divine, yet her prayers are considered so powerful that Orthodox Christians plead, "O most holy *Theotokos, save us.*" Some women have contended that the magnitude of the honor afforded to Mary places her so high above the rest of women that she is no longer one of us.[3] Yet such an assertion misses the point. Undeniably, Orthodox Christians reserve special honor for the *Theotokos* that they extend to no other saint; there is only one Virgin Mother of God. But the point here is that her womanhood does not prevent her from being the first among the millions of saints in the kingdom of God. And while her motherhood is an integral part of her sainthood, being a mother was not, in the eyes of the church, what made her a saint (as if a woman's value depends on her ability to biologically bear children). Rather, it was her humility and love of God that enabled her to respond: "Let it be to me according to your word" (Luke 1:38). This joyful discipleship, this perfect accord of the human and divine wills, is the paradigm for *all* Christians, women and men alike.

But for all the honor the church renders to the *Theotokos*, the fact remains that neither she nor any other woman presided over the eucharist or other sacraments of the Christian communities. The church teaches that the *Theotokos* was with the apostles at the coming of the Holy Spirit on Pentecost, and that she, along with the apostles, traveled to spread the Gospel beyond Jerusalem.[4] Other women, such as Sts. Mary Magdalen and Nina of Georgia, are known as equals-to-the-apostles. So, women have been spiritual leaders and preachers, but not bishops or priests.[5] One might speculate

---

participation in his life, while retaining the distinction between creature and Creator and the uniqueness of each person. He adeptly states that "the descent of the divine person of Christ makes human persons capable of an ascent in the Holy Spirit. It was necessary that the voluntary humiliation of the Son of God should take place, so that fallen men might accomplish their vocation, the deification of created beings by uncreated grace." Lossky, *In the Image and Likeness of God*, 97–98.

2. Hopko, "God and Gender," 160.

3. Topping, *Holy Mothers of Orthodoxy*, 8.

4. Holy Apostles Convent, *Life of the Virgin Mary*, 412; 429.

5. The question of whether the practice of women serving as deacons in the Orthodox Church is a related but distinct discussion from that of women's ordination to the episcopacy or priesthood. There is an historical precedent of women serving as deacons (though not in exactly the same manner as men), unlike the service of bishops or priests.

that the reason for this practice lay in the societal conventions of Judaic late antiquity; a woman would not have been accepted in the role of priest. However, various pagan cults with priestesses did exist at that time. Furthermore, an embattled Christian community that tossed aside the conventions of Jew/Gentile separation and embraced violent martyrdom as a glorious honor would not have simply lacked courage to defy social gender norms. So, were the apostles and all the generations of bishops simply interested in establishing and maintaining male control over this new community? Did they believe that doing so was their God-given duty? Again, women *did* hold certain positions of leadership and authority in the church, so why would such strong women have accepted malicious oppression?[6]

Fascinatingly, Orthodox scholars and theologians who have examined the question of the ordination of women to the priesthood have not come to a unanimous conclusion. Nevertheless, they *are* unanimous in the dogmatic assertion that women have the same intrinsic value as men as bearers of the image of God. But in the decades since the 1960s, when the World Council of Churches first broached the question of women's ordination, Orthodox scholars have engaged in a discussion about gender and priesthood that continues to this day. One of the two most fundamental points of contention in this discussion has proven to be whether the sexual differentiation in the human race functions as anything other than a means of reproduction. If the male/female duality in humanity is merely a means of reproduction, one could easily argue for the introduction of women to the priesthood, and a few Orthodox scholars have done so.[7] One lone scholar has expounded a unique argument for both understanding sexual duality's function as limited to reproduction *and* preserving the tradition of a male priesthood.[8] Yet other Orthodox scholars argue that while sexual duality certainly fulfills the function of reproduction, this is by no means the limit of that duality's significance in the human experience, suggesting that the

---

For an excellent study, see FitzGerald, *Women Deacons in the Orthodox Church*.

6. The assertion that the church has for over two millennia failed to properly perform priestly service by excluding women would seem to imply that Christian women were too weak, too blinded, or simply uninspired to take up the mantle of the priesthood. It also implies a failure on the part of God to convey his will concerning women and the priesthood to humanity.

7. Behr-Sigel, "Ordination of Women," 36; and Karras, "Panel on Personhood," 101–2.

8. Harrison, 1999, "Orthodox Arguments Against the Ordination of Women as Priests," 186

interaction between men and women is one of the ways by which we come to better know God.[9]

The other point of contention is the nature of the priesthood.[10] On the one hand, one can point to the orientation of the priest toward the people in the divine liturgy and argue that the priest is the icon of Christ—who is the one high priest (Heb 3:1; 5:9–10)—making Christ present to the church, and by virtue of this connection, the priest should be male.[11] On the other hand, one can point to the priest's orientation toward the altar and prayers on behalf of the church (which is spoken of in the feminine) as evidence that the priestly role is not tied exclusively or even primarily to the maleness of Christ or masculine relation of God to humanity.[12] The above summary, *perforce*, grossly oversimplifies this theological discussion, but one can sense even here the complexity of how the bishop/priest functions in the church, and how his maleness may or may not relate to the various facets of his role.

Finally, this discussion of the nature of men and women and the understanding of the priesthood began after World War II when Western society at large began confronting the disenfranchisement of women and their lack of various forms of power and authority. Scholars in the church have entered this discussion because the world has changed, and the Orthodox Church is not indifferent or immune to societal change. But it is critical to note that the question of power is not one which Orthodox spirituality recognizes as vital. The church teaches that those with power must use it judiciously, to protect the weak and help the poor, but it has never taught that those without power should seek it for themselves. Although filled with imperfect people who have fallen short of what it means to be fully human in God's image and likeness, the church understands the bishop or

---

9. Hopko, "Presbyter/Bishop," 158; and Behr, "Note on the Ontology of Gender," 370.

10. It is important to note the role of the priest in the Orthodox Church. While the priest can and does fulfill the role of preacher and spiritual counselor to his congregants, his most fundamental service is that of presiding over the eucharist, wherein the faithful are united into Christ's body by partaking of his body and blood. It is the bishop who presides over this liturgical act in the place of Christ, with the priests and deacons around him. In the parish community, the local priest serves with the bishop's blessing when the bishop, himself, cannot be present. Thus, it is the bishop who holds the fullness of the priesthood. See Aghiorgoussis, "Unity of the Church," 141–85.

11. Hopko, "Presbyter/Bishop," 158; and Harrison, "Orthodox Arguments Against the Ordination of Women," 184.

12. Behr-Sigel, "Ordination of Women," 36.

priest to be one who serves, one who lays down his life for the church. The Christian life is one in which we are called to embrace humility. Blessed are the poor in spirit—those who claim nothing as their own, nothing as their right. When Orthodox Christians consider whether the male priesthood epitomizes disdain and belittlement of women, the church confronts us with our own misunderstandings of the life to which God has called us—both here and in the hereafter.

When asked whether the Orthodox Church respects women, and whether the Orthodox Church ordains women to the priesthood, the church can respond with simple answers: yes, we esteem women, as we do men; and no, we do not ordain them to serve as priests. Then there are the complex answers that delve into the meaning of sexual duality, the nature of the priesthood, of human personhood, and the nature of God. Although the Church's position on these matters may seem contradictory and confusing to a modern American woman, the Church's daily life of worship and the reflections of Orthodox theologians provide ample opportunity for women to explore the many-faceted relationship between God and his children, whether male or female. As the discussion of the meaning of the priesthood and why God created men and women continues, those inquiring into the Orthodox faith can perhaps take comfort in knowing that the church has held fast to what has been handed down from the apostles, while at the same time practicing self-reflection and seeking ever to live in the here and now as the body of he who is the way, the truth, and the life.

10

Is Orthodoxy an Ethnically Exclusive Religion?

Fr. Ernesto Obregon

PERIODICALLY, I AM ASKED the question as to how I could be part of the Orthodox Church. After all, are not the Orthodox somewhat ethnically exclusive? I am not Slavic; I am not Greek; I am not Arab; how could I ever be accepted by the Orthodox? I suppose that I cannot blame people for thinking that. Let me be honest: I have experienced some Orthodox who have expressed this idea. I have even experienced some Orthodox hierarchs who have problems receiving Orthodox converts into the clergy because they do not speak the original language. And yet, I know of hierarchs in that same jurisdiction who do not have this reservation. So, what is the real Orthodoxy? Is it ethnically exclusive, or is the real Orthodoxy open to those who have not descended from traditionally Orthodox countries? A brief discussion of the Orthodox Church since the fall of the Ottoman Empire will lay a foundation for my answer.

In the late 1800s, the Bulgarians, Romanians, Greeks, etc., won their national independence from the Ottoman Turks, who had occupied their lands since the 1400s. For Orthodox Christians, this was a positive development that was quickly followed by a negative one. The positive development was that a people who had been unwillingly occupied by another people were now free to pursue their own national destiny. But there is always a danger when you win independence. The danger is that you will become overly proud of your distinct national background to the point where your nation's interests trump incomparably more important ones; including, in the particular case of Orthodox Christians, preserving the

Church's intercultural unity. Such conflation of church and nation is referred to as phyletism (or ethnophyletism), and was condemned as a heresy by a pan-Orthodox synod convened in 1872. This heretical tendency was particularly problematic for the church in the nineteenth century, but it started earlier.

Beginning with the French Revolution in the late eighteenth century, the philosophy of romantic nationalism spurred the transition from the old medieval kingdoms into the modern nation-state.[1] You no longer identified with the king, but with your ethnic/religious heritage. This transition caused problems not simply for the Orthodox Church, but also for other churches. Already, after the Reformation, the great Protestant state churches had formed. This process accelerated strongly during the eighteenth- to nineteenth-century transitions into the modern nation-state.

In the nineteenth century, this philosophy of romantic nationalism hit hard particularly in the Balkans. As new countries began to be carved out of parts of the Ottoman Empire, the dioceses inside those nations began to identify themselves more with the new nations rather than with the church/patriarchate as a whole, and the people began to identify themselves more with the church within their borders rather than with the church/patriarchate as a whole. National identification became even stronger if the new nation's existence was challenged by outside forces,[2] as was the case in Orthodox countries like Greece and Bulgaria, and Catholic countries like Ireland and Italy.

What few could have foreseen was Orthodoxy's subsequent expansion throughout the world. This expansion happened by way of emigration, rather than by way of missions. It was for economic reasons, not for evangelistic reasons. And because this expansion was not planned, it meant that many of the ethnic/nationalist/religious attitudes crossed into the New World from the original Orthodox areas, some of which were in the process of national renewal.

For most immigrants, religion formed part of their cultural self-identity, whether they were Eastern Orthodox, Roman Catholics, or Orthodox Jews. It was the religious group that helped to mediate their experience as new immigrants in a strange land while helping to maintain their identity. "Many scholars," Williams explains,

---

1. Nipperdey, "In Search of Identity," 11.
2. Mavrogordatos, "Orthodoxy and Nationalism in the Greek Case," 117–36.

Part 3—The Church and Her Teaching

> ... see the space of the church for immigrant communities as not only "insulating," but as "providing a secure social location from which [immigrant groups] can negotiate with greater success their identities and relations with others."[3]

I can now answer the question of whether Orthodoxy is an ethnically exclusive religion. Formally, the Eastern Orthodox Churches consider ethnic exclusivity to be a heresy. Were you to ask any bishop in any Orthodox Country, he would answer the same way. Converts must be not only welcomed, but actively sought. The church must, in addition, adapt to the country in which it finds itself, to include celebrating the divine liturgy in the language of the people. Clergy must be recruited not only from the descendants of the immigrants, but also from convert groups. But this is only a formal answer.

When national and religious identities are intertwined, as has been the case for many immigrants, it becomes difficult to accept converts (except by marriage) without calling into question the validity of one's national self-identity. The parish, through its cultural celebrations and its worship, which uses the language of the country of origin, reinforces the identity of the immigrant. The parish is a place of respite to which you can retreat when culture shock gets intense. Further, parish worship and social experience strengthen you to go out into this new world, knowing that you are not the only one who is experiencing the adjustment process. The parish is the place where your children (and grandchildren) learn about your origins and experience what you consider to be important beliefs and practices. The parish festival is a place where outsiders can acquire knowledge of you and your cultural heritage.

In this way, the immigrant parish easily becomes ethnically exclusive. The phyletism of the immigrant parish is not a deliberate violation of the ruling of the pan-Orthodox Council. It is not a denial or repudiation of what was said back then. Rather, it is a soul-deep belief that if the parish loses its ethnic identity, then its people will lose their ethnic identity. This makes it difficult for the immigrant parish to open itself to new incoming converts, lest they lose their identity. But this is not a problem that is exclusive to Eastern Orthodoxy. With respect to Hispanic Roman Catholic immigrants, it has been argued that

> many new immigrants are given a choice in U.S. society: maintain their language and culture as part of a subgroup of society,

---

3. Williams, *Christian Pluralism in the United States*, 274.

or conform to Anglo cultural norms in order to blend in and succeed. The family, school and workplace dynamics surrounding this choice often become pastoral issues in parishes, as the choice to assimilate or remain isolated in cultural pockets even becomes implicit in parish settings.[4]

Eastern Orthodox immigrant parishes in America also experience the conflict dynamics of whether to blend in or to be ethnically exclusive. Nevertheless, a parish cannot stay exclusive forever. Time, events or open discussion can and will change the exclusive orientation into a more open one. If the phyletism of a parish is not formal, but the natural result of the immigrant experience, then time will progressively take care of the problem with each new generation.

In some cases, Eastern Christian hierarchs are taking steps to educate their flocks. For instance, in the Coptic Orthodox Church in North America, the Coptic Pope has engaged his church in a discussion to ensure that it crosses the boundary from an immigrant church to an American church. His vision of the Coptic Church's future foresees measures that "include a shift in the language of prayers in immigrant churches to local languages," and "the ordination of priests that are either from the second generation or have been culturally localized in immigrant societies."[5]

Change will come; phyletism will recede. The current exclusivity expressed by some parishes is merely a stage in the transition from immigrant to American. Why am I Orthodox in spite of the phyletism of some parishes in America? Well, there are many reasons, Truth being among the most important. Another reason is the acceptance that I have received from parishioners even in traditionally phyletist parishes—an acceptance that confirms to me that this exclusivity is not a permanent feature. Thus, I have hope for a future of greater inclusivity in the Orthodox Church, both here in North America and the rest of the world.

---

4. Organ, "Immigrants and Inculturation."
5. Botros, *Competing for the Future*, ii.

PART 4

The Process of Salvation

11

The Problem of "Original Sin"

Fr. Panayiotis Papageorgiou

ONCE, A WOMAN CAME to my office to share with me the sadness that she had been experiencing for many years; she had had five miscarriages and was constantly mourning the loss of her children. Her biggest difficulty with the issue, however, was the belief that her children were condemned to hell because they were never baptized. She felt responsible for that and wondered how she could enter the kingdom of God after having committed so many sins when her babies, who never saw the light of day, ended up in hell. I asked her how she had come to that conclusion, and she answered that she was taught early in her life that all people—even infants—who die and were never baptized go to hell because of "original sin."

Many Christian groups continue to teach that there is a transmission of the sin and guilt of Adam from parents to children (and the pastoral consequences of this doctrine have not yet been seriously considered). Baptism is usually offered as the way to cleanse the person from this sin and guilt. Furthermore, it is usually taught that the consequence of this sin and guilt is condemnation to eternal hell, even for infants, unless they have been baptized.

A serious pastoral problem is created by this doctrine when faced with the death of an unbaptized child, especially a child of baptized and faithful parents. Two questions arise from this: (1) How can baptized parents transmit to their children sin and guilt from which they themselves have been cleansed?, and (2) How can a just and merciful God condemn a child that has no sins of his/her own for the sin of someone else, especially the sin of someone so far removed from them in time?

Part 4—The Process of Salvation

Historically speaking, the concept of original sin was propagated through the centuries in the Western Christian world. They received this teaching from the great saint and doctor, Augustine of Hippo, who had based his anthropology on the concept of "traducianism."[1] According to this concept, human souls, like human bodies, are derived from the seed of the father, hence the father may transmit to his children even his own sins. This idea is clearly found in Tertulian and Ambrosiaster's[2] commentaries on Romans, which were written during the papacy of Damasus (366–84). Augustine was influenced in his theory of human nature by both Ambrose and Ambrosiaster. It was Ambrosiaster's commentary, however, that played a decisive role in Augustine's theory of "original sin." It was here that Augustine discovered not only the traducianist concept but also the idea of sinning *in massa*; that is, that the whole human race has sinned through Adam and is condemned through his sin. This was not the understanding, however, among the Greek-speaking Eastern Christian fathers and theologians of the church.

It is well known that Augustine knew little Greek,[3] and he seems to have failed to clearly understand the teaching of the Greek fathers who lived before him. Even though he had read some of the texts, which should have corrected his teaching on this issue, he failed to reach the same conclusions.[4]

Augustine believed that all human beings have sinned in Adam *in massa* and are thus condemned along with him. He also believed that the fallen human condition and the original sin of Adam *has defiled (contaminavit)* all humanity and that this defilement is propagated through the act of procreation. Furthermore, he believed and taught that every human being born into the world inherits through the seed of his father the sin and

---

1. Bonner argues that, according to Augustine, "Adam's primal sin is passed on to his descendants as a kind of hereditary infection, which Augustine on one occasion compares to gout . . . So the sin which was voluntary in Adam becomes natural in his descendants." Bonner, "Augustine's Theology on 'Adam,'" col. 82. See also Wiles, *Making of Christian Doctrine*, 55.

2. This is an unknown writer from the fourth century, whom St. Augustine erroneously thought to be St. Ambrose of Milan, and thus treated his writings as authoritative. Because of this, modern scholars named him "Ambrosiaster" (which literally means "would-be Ambrose" in Latin).

3. In his *Confessions*, Augustine reveals that he had difficulty with, and in fact despised, the Greek language.

4. See Papageorgiou, "Chrysostom and Augustine on the Sin of Adam," 361–78.

guilt of Adam—the "original sin"—and is thus condemned to hell, unless he/she is baptized.

On the Eastern side of the church, St. John Chrysostom, a contemporary of Augustine, followed the tradition of the Greek fathers before him, and saw the transgression of Adam as the cause of our present fallen condition, whereby all are bound by weaknesses, shame, fear, suffering, "many natural shortcomings" (πολλά φυσικά ελαττώματα), and above all, by death. Chrysostom believed that we have all been consigned to this condition, though not as a punishment, but rather out of the mercy and providence of God. Not only did we not lose from this condition, he claims, but in fact we have gained. This condition has become for us a training ground (διδασκαλείον) for virtue, so that we may become capable of receiving the future gifts of God. Chrysostom rejects the idea that we are responsible for and being punished for Adam's sin as absurd. We are only responsible, he explains, for the sins we commit ourselves willingly (οίκοθεν).

With regard to baptism, Chrysostom agrees with infant baptism, not because there is a need to cleanse a child from the sin and guilt of Adam, or because infants have sins of their own, but because through baptism they will receive sanctification, justification, sonship, inheritance, brotherhood with Christ, and become members of Christ and a dwelling place for the Holy Spirit. He says nothing about the forgiveness of Adam's sin, of which a child has supposedly inherited the guilt. In fact, nowhere in the texts that I have examined, including those quoted or referred to by Augustine in *Contra Julianum Palagianum*,[5] have I found anything in Chrysostom's writings suggesting the propagation of the "first sin" through the act of procreation.

From the examination of the text of *Contra Julianum*, it seems to me that Augustine had read these same texts, but either misunderstood or completely ignored the passages that clearly explicated the position of Chrysostom on the issue. The reason for this was probably because he was already convinced of the correctness of his own belief. It is also possible that he thought he was protecting the memory of St. John from a possible association with the Pelagian heresy (there are some indications of this in his comments). In doing so, however, he established in the West a teaching of "original sin" not completely in line with the patristic tradition (at least that of the East), which was to have a lasting effect on the Western church, being accepted by Roman Catholic and Protestant theologians alike up to our time.

5. Augustine, *Contra Julianum Pelagianum*.

Part 4—The Process of Salvation

There are obviously serious intellectual difficulties with Augustine's teaching. As Gerald Bonner points out:

> It is not clear by what justice humanity can share in Adam's guilt when it existed only in potentiality in his loins at the time of the Fall. It is also difficult to see why the children of the baptized should inherit a guilt from which their parents have been cleansed. Finally, it has been argued that Pope Zosimus' condemnation of Pelagianism in his *Tractoria* did not constitute a complete endorsement of the Canon's of Carthage of 418, which represent Augustine's doctrine in its most rigorous form.[6]

In other words, Bonner, a Roman Catholic Theologian, questions this doctrine on three levels: the injustice inherent in the concept of original sin, the lack of consideration of the effects of baptism on parents, and finally, its legality.

I would like to take this a step further and point to an important modern theological development in the West, which has its roots in Augustine's doctrine of original sin; this is the more recent doctrine-made-dogma of the "Immaculate Conception" of the Virgin Mary. It seems to me that it was mainly the need of Roman Catholic theology to cleanse the Mother of God from Augustine's "inherited guilt" that led to the proclamation and final establishment of this new dogma. Had this notion of transmission of defilement and guilt from Adam to his descendants not been so strong in the West, there would have been no need for such a theological development.

Conclusion

I offered the lady who had the five miscarriages the theology of St. John Chrysostom as a more reasonable alternative to what she had known so far and which was so troubling to her. I explained that God is just and would never condemn anyone for someone else's sin. I argued that if human judges, who are sinful and imperfect, would never do such a thing, how could God, who is the supreme source of all justice. I pointed to St. Chrysostom's reassurance that children are innocent and God receives them as such: In Homily 28 on Matthew, he quotes Sophia Sirah 3:1—"the souls of the just

---

6. Bonner, "Augustine's Theology on 'Adam,'" col. 83.

are in the hand of God"—and concludes that "so also are the souls of children, for they also are not wicked."[7]

The woman left with a smile on her face. She found peace and comfort in this more reasonable teaching of the Eastern fathers of the church.

---

7. Chrysostom, "Homily 28 on Matthew," 341.

12

Are We Saved by Faith Alone? The Orthodox View on the Doctrine of Sola Fide

Fr. Steven Ritter

IF PEOPLE TODAY CAN understand the impact that a man like Thomas Edison had on the human race—changing forever the face of the world and the way that all of us live—then it is not such a stretch to agree with the axiom that one person in the right historical period can indeed effect a tidal wave on Christian history. Martin Luther did just that, and the waters have still not receded.

It all began with this verse, the rallying cry of the Reformation: "Therefore we conclude that a man is justified by faith apart from the deeds of the law" (Rom 3:28). It took a long time for this foundational statement from St. Paul to twist and turn in Martin Luther's mind, and his ruminations in his *Lectures on Romans* in 1515 provide only the smallest hints of the revolution his thought would spark. St. Paul haunted the psychologically tormented Augustinian monk; he desperately searched the Scriptures in order to find answers to those questions which left him dazed and insecure, completely unsure of his standing before God, unable to meet what he believed (falsely) were the impossible standards of piety imposed upon a Christian. And he labored under the mistaken idea that the Roman Catholicism of the time was a religion purely driven by "works" in opposition to "faith"; though the medieval Western church could often be unclear about this aspect of the Christian life, and abuses and scandals abounded, Luther's failure to grasp the entirety of the Christian tradition sprang mostly from his own inner needs and personality. In these early lectures, Luther taught that "God wraps himself in mystery and reveals himself only to the elect, whose election is certified by torments such as those Luther himself has experienced."[1]

Sola fide, or faith alone, was one of the three pinnacles of Luther's reformation: along with the others, *sola gratia* (grace alone) and *sola scriptura* (Scriptures alone), this doctrine forms part of the theory that we are released from our sins and made righteous by grace, through faith, on the basis of what is clearly indicated in Scripture. But does scripture "clearly" express this idea? While there are numerous references that can be interpreted in this manner when taken apart from the whole, there are an equal number of passages that seem to indicate just the opposite. Luther himself, caught in this quandary, sought to solve part of the problem by inserting the word "alone" into Romans 3:28 in his edition of the German bible (so we are justified by faith *alone*), a work he revised his entire life, and which was crafted to support his own theological opinions (in some editions, the word "alone" was even printed in a larger font!). He reasoned as follows: "The text itself and the meaning of St. Paul urgently require and demand it. For in that very passage he [Paul] is dealing with the main point of Christian doctrine, namely, that we are justified by faith in Christ without any works of the Law."[2]

Aside from the amazing assertion that Paul is somehow unclear about the matter, does this passage warrant the unscriptural addition? The fact is that it was added specifically not to clarify Paul, but to contradict James, who says, "You see then that a man is justified by works, and not by faith only" (Jas 2:24). Most Christians today—through no fault of their own—find themselves caught in the same sort of intellectual confusion that trapped Luther. The idea that the work of justification is entirely of God, having nothing to do with us, misses Paul's broader vision. As Fr. Georges Florovsky explained, "St. Paul uses language that would be meaningless if man were merely a passive object in the redemptive process, if justification by faith was an action that took place only on the divine level."[3] Luther, however was getting way off track partly because of his overreliance on the works of St. Augustine, which he did not entirely understand:

> More than a thousand years before Luther's Reformation, St. Augustine had said, "For my part, I should not believe the Gospel except as moved by the authority of the catholic Church." For him,

1. Marius, *Martin Luther*, 109.
2. Lindberg, *European Reformations*, 49.
3. Florovsky, *Byzantine Ascetic and Spiritual Fathers*, 34.

PART 4—THE PROCESS OF SALVATION

as for the other Fathers of the early church, the truth of the Gospel was confirmed by the living experience of the Church, which is Christ's very body upon earth, animated by the Holy Spirit. Luther, however, turned St. Augustine's theology of the Church on its head.[4]

One of the problems in dealing with the doctrine of *sola fide* is that proponents are not all in agreement as to what it means. Some see our justification as a one-time event where its effects are never lost, while others admit to the possibility of loss of faith and consequently, of justification. Many believe in imparted righteousness while others believe, more similar to the Orthodox, that this righteousness must be maintained by living lives of holiness. The similarity ends there—even those who agree to the possibility of losing justification still believe that it is given to us in a legal manner, in the way God looks at us, cloaking us in him, while the Orthodox Church steadfastly maintains that our righteousness, while originating in God, transforms and renews us, resulting not merely in a changed legal verdict, but in an actual change in our nature, making us new creatures in Christ. The birth of the idea that faith alone is sufficient as to all things regarding salvation is ultimately tied to the very notion of the authority of the church, which teaches our justification in Christ to be the *beginning* of our salvation (at baptism) that leads us step by step to union with Christ. It is *not* just a legal action on the part of the Savior, the *sine qua non* of classical Reformation teaching. Using the text of Romans 3:28 as if it were the foundational verse of all Christian theology robs the original passage of its meaning, which is given in the context of Paul's arguing against the Jews and their insistence on works of the law of Moses as "justifying." Luther tends to equate works of the Law with efforts of spiritual progress of *any* kind, radically advancing the idea that salvation is obtained and imputed to us without any "actual" change taking place in the human person, the very reason for the incarnation. Such a notion is found nowhere in the tradition of the church, and, importantly, nowhere in the Scriptures themselves. Indeed, this doctrine subverts the teaching of the Lord, himself: "If you love me, keep my commandments" (John 14:15).

This confusing of works of the Law with any effort in regards to the spiritual life in Christ had devastating effects on Christian theology, reducing the premise of "putting on Christ" to mere poetical allegory. For if our putting on Christ is merely *his putting himself on us*, then our obedience

---

4. Carlton, *The Way*, 193.

to the call to "follow him" becomes optional, unrelated to our salvation. One does not only accept the justification that comes from faith, but must continue by means of good, *spiritual* works, not to *earn* salvation, but to assimilate the grace freely given, and continue to train and mold his new nature into the likeness of the Lord. Gifts must be accepted, and then *used* in order to be of any profit. And we can refuse them at any time. So the Lord grants us, through faith, admission into his kingdom, and we can stay as long as we want! But we do have to desire to be there, and no one forcibly keeps us there against our will by an irresistible grace. The kingdom begins *now*, and this life is the time when we prepare ourselves for the everlasting portion by learning to love the Lord in purity and truth, and really becoming like him by grace. St. Paul writes, "Therefore consider the goodness and severity of God: on those who fell, severity; but toward you, goodness, *if* you continue in his goodness. Otherwise, you also will be cut off" (Rom 11:22, emphasis added). St. John similarly shows the fallacy of thinking that a person can be justified while not following the narrow path, and the stringency of his words is worth noting:

> If we say that we have fellowship with Him, and walk in darkness, we lie and do not practice the truth. But *if* we walk in the light as He is in the light, we have fellowship with one another, and the blood of Jesus Christ His son cleanses us from all sin. (1 John 1:6–7, emphasis added)

In his reply to Lutheran theologians from Tübingen, who sought approval of their newly fashioned Augsburg Confession, Orthodox Patriarch Jeremiah II wrote the following:

> We do not merely say that those who obey the law shall be justified, but those who obey the spiritual law, which is understood spiritually and according to the inner man . . . you contend that, as you believe, the remission of sins is granted mainly by faith alone. But the Church demands a living faith, which is made evident by good works . . . furthermore, Basil the Great says: "The grace from above does not come to the one who is not striving. But both of them, the human endeavor and the assistance descending from above through faith, must be mixed together for the perfection of virtue."[5]

If, indeed, justification by faith alone means being made righteous by faith alone, with nothing else required on our ends, then we can see

5. Mastrantonis, *Augsburg and Constantinople*, 178.

that righteousness is not necessarily connected to those acts that the Lord considers God-pleasing (and by which we shall all be judged)—feeding the hungry, clothing the naked, visiting the sick and those in prison—or our ongoing tendency to sin. In this context one can live one's life pretending to be righteous while continuing to sin every minute of the day. This makes Christian life an absurdity, and the entire moral instruction of the Lord in the Gospels simply suggestions as to how to live a good life—we see the fruits of this belief in many popular preachers today—instead of saving and mandatory ordinances which leaven our *path* to salvation.

13

The Three-Fold Way

Kyriacos C. Markides

I WILL TRY TO show in this brief chapter that in the monasteries of Eastern Orthodoxy, perhaps more so than in any other part of the Christian world, a healing mystical tradition has been preserved that we assumed was only prevalent in religions like Hinduism, Tibetan Buddhism and Native American shamanism. Many Westerners, disenchanted with the prevailing rationalism of mainstream culture, both in terms of its scientific as well as its religious expression, turned toward the Far East for an experiential and mystical pathway to Reality. Unbeknown to them, such a pathway has always existed within Christianity, particularly in its Eastern, "Byzantine" expression.

I would also like to suggest that the increasing interest among modern people in "paranormal" and miraculous phenomena (angels, prophetic visions, out-of-body travel, near-death experiences, extraordinary healings, etc.) dismissed by doctrinaire skeptics as non-phenomena, have been the *sin qua non* of the life of Eastern Orthodox saints and a hallmark of Eastern Orthodox sacred tradition. Therefore, the mystical culture of Eastern Christianity should be of interest not only to mainstream Christians of all denominations but also to an increasing number of Westerners who have been attracted to the religions of the Far East and their New Age variants, a trend that has become so much a part of our cultural and religious landscape today.

The hallmark of Eastern Orthodox spirituality is what I have called, as a result of my twenty-year investigation, *The Three-Fold Way*.[1] The holy

---

1. See Markides, *Mountain of Silence*; Markides, *Gifts of the Desert*; and Markides,

Part 4—The Process of Salvation

elders teach that the reestablishment of the shattered unity between human beings and God proceeds in three identifiable stages: *Catharsis* (the purification of the soul), *Fotisis* (the enlightenment or illumination of the soul) and *Theosis* (union with God). These stages, which I will summarize below, are considered by the holy elders of the Christian East to be the universal, necessary and fundamental stages that all human beings must traverse before they reunite with God, the ultimate healing and salvation of the individual soul and its final destination.

The premise upon which *The Three-Fold Way* stands is the axiom that human beings since time immemorial have fallen from grace. They have shattered their connection with God and live their lives in a state of exile from their true homeland. This is the meaning of "original sin" according to the holy elders of Eastern Christianity. A key precondition for union with God implies deep *metanoia, a* radical change of heart and mind, which will initiate the process of *Catharsis*, or the purification of the soul from egotistical passions. The story of Genesis in the Old Testament and the parable of the prodigal son in the New Testament allude to this fundamental existential truth about human origins and destiny. In Jesus' parable, the prince left the palace of the loving father and cut himself off from his spiritual roots. He then squandered his divine inheritance by indulging in the various passions and temptations of the material world. His entire human nature was distorted and the powers that were given to him as instruments to contemplate his creator were now employed for the satisfaction of egotistical passions. For example, the capacity of the soul for anger as a force to resist temptation and sin became a source for discord among humans—both individually and collectively—in pursuit of worldly goals. Similarly, pride in one's divine lineage degenerated into an obsession for owning material things and craving for fame and power over others.

At a certain point, the prodigal son is exhausted from his unsavory existence (which is life cut off from God) and begins to yearn for the palace of the loving father. This is the beginning of the return journey. The prodigal after great difficulties and tribulations to overcome his narcissism and destructive passions and addictions eventually returns to his true homeland. The compassionate and forgiving father embraces him, orders a feast to celebrate his return and offers him the ring of eternity. The palace, that is, the inner kingdom, is always part of us but we do not recognize it because it is covered up by poor habits, inattention, and exclusive focus on

---

Inner River.

the material world. The Prodigal Son never stops being a prince even while living among the pigs (notice the structural similarities of the prodigal son story, Plato's parable of the cave, Odysseus' return to Ithaca and Prince Gautama's sojourn away from his father's palace until his "enlightenment" under the Bo tree).

The Christian elders teach that the process of return and the healing and restoration of the soul to its original divine state requires arduous spiritual struggles and effort. It is a point often lost on a culture that values effortless pursuits and instant gratification. On the basis of the experiences and teachings of its great saints and holy elders, the *Ecclesia*[2] provides a methodology on how to heal the soul, how to free oneself from egotistical desires, and how to reestablish union with God. This methodology is called *askesis*, which literally means exercise. The full-time practitioners of *askesis* are the ascetics, the spiritual marathon runners whose practices and discoveries can help those of us who live in the world continue on our journey home.

Among the set of practices that form *askesis* are regular participation in the sacraments of the *Ecclesia* including confession, communion, charitable action in the world, fasting, ceaseless prayer, systematic study of sacred texts and the lives of the saints, cultivation of deep humility, all-night vigils and communal worship. Charity, when given freely and unselfconsciously, is important in all of its material and non-material facets as a means of forgetting our own self-absorption and our tendency to imprison our hearts and minds to the things of this world. Similarly, fasting trains the soul to master the lower passions. The logic behind it is that unless you gradually learn to overcome small temptations, such as avoidance of certain foods, you will not develop the power to resist greater temptations that unavoidably assault our everyday existence. Confession, through the spiritual guidance of an experienced elder, is also essential so that we not only address our sinful actions, but, most importantly, we can become conscious and thus monitor our *logismoi*, the negative thought-forms that we constantly generate in our mind and that deposit layer upon layer of separation between us and God. We are called to replace these *logismoi* with systematic and ceaseless remembrance and contemplation of God

---

2. The *Ecclesia* refers to "the sum total of the practices, methods, sacred texts, and the testimony of saints and their teachings on how to know God. It includes the organization structure of the Church. The *Ecclesia* is seen as a spiritual hospital for the cure of the maladies of the heart that obstruct our vision of God." Markides, *Mountain of Silence*, 251.

through prayer. A most important practice is the incessant repetition of short prayers, foremost of which is the *Noera Prosefche*, or the Jesus Prayer ("Lord Jesus Christ, Son of God, have mercy of me, a sinner"). The practitioner is advised to repeat this prayer as much as possible. It can be recited even while engaging in monotonous worldly activities, like waiting at a bus stop or washing dishes. The purpose of this practice is to minimize the creation of negative thought-forms and replace them with the memory of God as a vehicle to recapture the paradisiacal stage, which can be attained in one's present life. For the holy elders, the Jesus Prayer is an invocation of the Holy Name that in conjunction with reciting long-established prayers like the Psalms, reading about the lives of saints and attending regular communal services, eventually will bear fruit in the life of the practitioner.[3]

At a certain point, for the soul that engages in purifying *askesis* for the overcoming of worldly passions, *Fotisis* (illumination) will follow. At this stage, when the soul has undergone its purification and attained depths of humility, divine providence offers the soul extraordinary gifts such as the experience of the "Uncreated Light" (God's light), prophetic vision, healing abilities, "paranormal" phenomena of levitation, bi-location and the like. These gifts are deeply buried within human nature and, as a rule, become manifest as gifts of grace after the soul's purification. Therefore, what we call "paranormal" phenomena are in reality very normal at this second stage of the soul's journey to God. These are the gifts that are reported in the lives of saints, who serve as models for us of what we may become.

As far as the saints are concerned, the gift of the Spirit that supersedes all others is the vision of the Uncreated Light, the mystical contemplation of God's presence in the world that floods the soul with exquisite joy. The following is a typical example of such an experience, as narrated by Elder Joseph from the Vatopaedi monastery of Mount Athos:

> I remember clearly that as soon as I began to mention the name of Christ several times in my prayer my heart filled with love. Suddenly it increased so much that I was no longer praying, but was in a state of wonder about this overflowing of love. I wanted to embrace and kiss all human beings and the entire creation, and, at the same time, I was thinking so humbly . . . I felt the presence of our Christ, but I could not see Him. I wanted to fall down to His immaculate feet and ask Him how does He set fire to the hearts of people and yet remain hidden from them. I was then given to

---

3. There are variants of the Jesus Prayer, such as the one devised by Saint Gregory Palamas, who used to pray "Lord Enlighten my Darkness" over and over.

understand that Christ is inside every human being. I said, my Lord let me be in this state forever and I need nothing else.

He further has this to say on the matter:

When the mind of the person has been cleansed, purified and enlightened . . . it is given, in addition to its own light, the light of Divine Grace so that it remains permanently within him. Then it snatches him and exposes him to visions and perceptions true to Its own nature. However, such a person has the capacity, if he so wishes, to ask for them through prayer. Then Grace is energized and what he asks for is given simply because he asks. But I believe the truly devout avoid such requests except in extraordinary circumstances.[4]

As Elder Joseph states, those who are offered such gifts of the Spirit accept them in utter humility, and must never be a source for self-promotion and self-aggrandizement. In fact, such gifts may become strong temptations that can often lead to a spiritual fall. That is why great saints do their utmost to hide them and use them only sparingly and only to help fellow human beings in their spiritual, psychological and medical needs. It is for this reason, also, that the desert fathers have been called *nyptic* (or vigilant). They were constantly fully conscious and on guard against such temptations. Therefore, from the point of view of the holy elders of Orthodoxy, any healing, prophetic or other unusual ability that one may be endowed with should not be flaunted for the sake of impressing an audience, as happens so often today among certain "New Age" circles. I remember the strong reaction of the late Elder Paisios, a holy hermit from Mt. Athos, when I naively asked him about his reputed abilities to heal people. He emphatically denied such "rumors," stating that all he does is pray for people and that whatever healing takes place is the result of God's grace and providence. Yet these rumors crossed the Atlantic, reaching me in Maine when I first heard of him and of his reputed friendship with wild animals like bears and poisonous snakes (in Orthodox spirituality the God-realized individual who has reached paradise in this life reestablishes a harmonious relationship with nature, which was characteristic of life before the fall. Hence the legends of saints who lived among wild beasts without fear of being harmed).

Finally, the third stage in one's spiritual development is the attainment of *Theosis*, the final destination of the human soul and its restoration into the oneness of God. It is the ultimate healing of the soul. As with the

4. Quoted in Markides, *Riding with the Lion*, 302–3.

previous stage of *Fotisis*, it is totally in the hands of grace. Human beings cannot reunite with God strictly on their own accord. Our will must be engaged only at the first stage (i.e., *Catharsis*). The other two stages follow naturally as God's rewards, as it were, for our struggles to purify our hearts and minds. Therefore attempts to get to those "gifts" directly (e.g., trying to develop one's psychic powers) without at the same time struggling to free the soul from egotism may be the equivalent of "stealing from God," leading to what has been called "black magic."

All of the great sages have pointed out that uniting with God in *Theosis* is ineffable, and therefore beyond all human description or comprehension. I should also point out that, in Christian spirituality, the soul upon its return home maintains its autonomy within the oneness of God. The self-conscious "I" does not get diluted into the All. What is annihilated is the sum total of our egotistical passions and desires, not our uniqueness as self-conscious beings created in the image and likeness of God for eternity. The God-realized human being will retain his or her uniqueness within the Oneness of God while continuing from the paradisiacal side to work for the salvation of others. It is also important to repeat that *Theosis* is not a stage that one can reach only after death, but also while one is still alive and active in this world. The paradisiacal stage is possible from this side of the divide. Our paradise or our hell can start from the here and now.

14

Once Saved, Always Saved?

Joshua Packwood

THE GOAL OF ORTHODOXY is salvation. The attainment of this goal is not something that one does by merit—it is a gift from God. Thus, if one is "saved" by the grace of God, then it would seem to follow that, after one has been baptized or confessed Jesus Christ as Lord and Savior, salvation would be final. After all, if salvation is God's and not one's own doing, then what could one do to be "unsaved"?

For Orthodox Christians, however, salvation is not completed by a single event of grace. Rather grace is given constantly throughout one's life. Moreover, this grace is given in conjunction with one's desire and acts in conformity with the love of God. That is to say, free will enables us to accept or reject God's grace. If one responds favorably to God, then one cooperates or participates in the divine activity of grace. This cooperative activity between human beings and God is called synergy. Synergy is simply the joining of human beings with the activities of their Creator, in the process of redemption or salvation. As St. Paul says in 1 Corinthians 39, "we are God's fellow workers [*synergoi*]."

In order to get a better view of this cooperative redemption, let us look at three different ways that the Scriptures refer to salvation. First, salvation is seen as something that has happened. Christ's victory over death is definitive and complete. For example, "The one who believes and is baptized will be saved; but the one who does not believe will be condemned." This salvation is accomplished by Christ's life, death, resurrection, and it is completed by one's baptism into the Christian faith.

Part 4—The Process of Salvation

The second conception of salvation is employed in the present tense, and refers to a process in which the Christian is currently and directly involved in their salvation. It is exemplified in 1 Corinthians 15: 1–2:

> Moreover, brethren, I declare to you the gospel which I preached to you, which also you received and in which you stand, by which also you are saved, if you hold fast that word which I preached to you—unless you believed in vain.[1]

"Being saved" is conditional. In this passage St. Paul is arguing that salvation is dependent on "holding fast" to the message; otherwise the belief is in vain. Thus, salvation is not complete for the individual simply by believing a proposition at one moment in time; one is not secure in their salvation unless they *continue* to fast to this message.

The following passage from Philippians 2:12–13 further elucidates the notion of being saved:

> Therefore, my beloved, as you have always obeyed, not as in my presence only, but now much more in my absence, work out your own salvation with fear and trembling; for it is God who works in you both to will and to do for His good pleasure.

Here St. Paul is encouraging readers to obey his teachings, which is the way in which one "works out" their salvation. Salvation, then, is a process in which one participates with God. One should note, however, that this participation in salvation (with "fear and trembling") is not something the Christian is doing on their own. Rather the readers must notice the emphasis on the working of God. It is God working through the Christian that enables salvation.

This mysterious, present sense of salvation refers to Christ being active in the life of the Christian. As St. Paul says in Colossians 1:27, "To them God willed to make known what are the riches of the glory of this mystery among the Gentiles: which is Christ in you, the hope of glory." He further expounds on this mystery in the following verses:

> Him we preach, warning every man and teaching every man in all wisdom, that we may present every man perfect in Christ Jesus. To this end I also labor, striving according to His working which works in me mightily. (Col 1:28–29)

---

1. See also 1 Cor 1:18.

Thus, salvation is not something which is done and completed by holding to a particular set of beliefs. Rather, it is "labor." That is to say, salvation encompasses all that the Christian is, not merely some intellectual assent to propositional beliefs. We are constantly engaged in this labor throughout our lives.

Finally, we have salvation in the future tense. Christ's prophecy of persecution most succinctly illustrates this final element of salvation. The most poignant passage is probably Matthew 24:10–13, in which Christ, referring to those who have believed but will not endure in the faith, states,

> And then many will be offended, will betray one another, and will hate one another. Then many false prophets will rise up and deceive many. And because lawlessness will abound, the love of many will grow cold. *But he who endures to the end shall be saved.* (emphasis added)

What we find here is an emphasis on salvation as a future act that is not to be taken for granted. The Christian must endure *in order to be* saved. This passage should stir up Christians for the obvious implication of the lack of security in one's own salvation.

Salvation is indeed a mystery and paradox in the same way that many things are mysterious in the Christian faith. It is not solely what has happened or is currently happening, but also what will happen. To overemphasize one conception of salvation over the other is to betray ignorance of this mystery. In short, Orthodox Christianity does not accept a "once saved, always saved" theology. At no moment is salvation ever complete. It is not something that one gets and never loses. Rather, it must be obtained and *maintained* with the humility embodied in the Jesus Prayer: "Lord Jesus Christ, Son of God, have mercy on me, a sinner."

PART 5

Toward *Theosis*: An Introduction to Orthodox Asceticism

15

Is Asceticism Just an "Eastern Thing"?

James J. Miller

BLACK CLOTH, ASHES, STILLNESS, and the stern life—all descriptions often associated with asceticism. Images of strange places, large monasteries, and strict practice dominate popular media representations of asceticism, making it seem distant and foreign. In our consumerist culture, asceticism seems all the more irrelevant. While it may be easiest to spot asceticism in Far Eastern traditions like Buddhism or Hinduism, asceticism is not restricted to these religions. Asceticism is actually more common in our daily lives than we recognize. It is a theme and underlining assumption of the New Testament. For Christians, the question is not *whether* one should practice asceticism, but *how*.

For such ancient thinkers as the Greeks and Romans, asceticism was a path to beauty and freedom. The term asceticism comes from the Greek term *askesis*, which is often translated as training or exercise, making it hard to see the connection to asceticism in many texts. Philosophy itself was understood as a form of *askesis*. Competing in the Olympic games was viewed as a metaphor for the way one should strive to wisdom, how one must train, and this was done through practices like abstinence, distancing, physical practices, and mental exercises—as explicated in the writings of Porphyry, Plato, the Stoics, and the Cynics. What is important to note is not the particular practices, but the goals of those practices. *Askesis* was regarded as the pathway to happiness and joy.[1] Further, these were not purely religious practices (indeed, practice, religion, and philosophy were

---

1. Ware, "Way of the Ascetics," 4.

Part 5—Toward *Theosis*

difficult to distinguish within their *askesis*), but ways in which one ordered his life and thoughts.

The point should be made that asceticism is not restricted to specialized religious narratives, people, or practices. By reading the works of Michal Foucault and Richard Valantasis one can understand asceticism more specifically as a self-forming practice that is oriented toward a *telos*, or goal. People undergo practices every day that they hope will bring about a change in their bodies, relationships, or their "selves." People deny themselves fatty foods to lose weight, cultivate virtues like kindness in the hopes of being better people, and seek to reach future goals through acts like saving money. All of these things tend to revolve around the person we wish to become. It is the particular change and formation of the self or subjectivity that differentiates asceticism from generalized goal attainment.

Asceticism also carries a cultural significance. When differentiating cultures, one tends to talk about their unique practices and customs. Purposefully taking on a set of practices to become a part of a culture can thus be understood as a form of asceticism. This is the basic idea that lead Geoffrey Harpham to claim that asceticism is the basic MS-DOS or operating system of culture.[2] Valantasis takes this a step further and claims that it is ascetic practice that not only distinguishes cultures but what integrates people into those cultures and allows them to separate or create new subjectivities or ways of being. Thus asceticism is not only about self-formation, but about the creation and maintenance of the community in which one seeks to be integrated. It is through ascetic practices that one is able to deconstruct the old-self and reconstruct a new one;[3] or, to put it another way, "to put off the old man" and "put on the new" (Col 3: 19–20).

Thus far we can see that asceticism has roots in Western thought via the Greeks and Romans, is a part of our culture, and creates a way of living and community. If asceticism is necessary to goal attainment, self-formation, and being a part of a culture or group, the question again is not whether one should practice asceticism, but how. The answer to the latter question is what Christians have been working out for some two thousand years. Many religions include such practices as fasting, prayer, and liturgical worship: what makes Christian asceticism different from other forms is

---

2. Harpham, *Ascetic Imperative in Culture and Criticism*, xi.
3. Valantasis, "Making of the Self."

the particular *telos* toward which these practices are oriented: union with Christ.[4]

Asceticism is not a late development in Christianity; to the contrary, not only does the word *askesis* appear in the New Testament (Acts 24:16), the entire New Testament assumes asceticism as a basic spiritual process. New Testament writers make extensive use of the ascetic Greek metaphor of the athlete to describe the Christian life (later writers on asceticism utilized these metaphors and Greek terms[5]). Ascetic themes like self-denial (Matt 16:24), self-control (2 Pet 1:6; 1 Thess 4:4), celibacy (1 Cor 7:25–35), and living in community (Acts 4:32–37) can be seen throughout the parables and epistles, and their connections become much more apparent in the original Greek. Ascetic practices and thought give form to these imperatives. Jesus assumes that we will fast, and gives guidance on doing so (Matt 6:16). Every Christian tradition includes practices and codes of conduct that are intended to bring about spiritual benefit or change, or to set them apart as Christians, whether they explicitly call these ascetic or not.

Since the goal for Christians is Christ and his kingdom, as much as there is a role for restrictions, separation, and self-denial, these are not ends in themselves. Christian ascetical writers warn against viewing one's fasting, prayers, or other ascetical practices as the end; Jesus chastises the leaders of his day for such legalism. Notice that Jesus does not critique such pharisaic practices as fasting or prayer, but in making the quality and visibility of those practices paramount. Putting asceticism above the goal of union with Christ would be akin to seeing training as the goal and forgetting the contest or race itself (cf. 1 Cor 9). One prays to commune with God, not to become more eloquent in prayer.

It is important to understand that asceticism, like Christianity itself, is voluntary. One always has the choice as to whether to pray, fast, become a monk, refrain from sin, or sell his possessions. Therefore, ascetic practices are seen as gifts—not obligations imposed on us—because they are ways to overcome barriers to the spiritual life and become more authentically human. Therefore, Christian asceticism is more concerned about transfiguring the person than purveying rules on proper moral conduct. It is both

---

4. *Theosis* (or deification) is another way of discussing the *telos* of man, or union with God through grace. This process is also inseparable from life in community, as God himself is Trinity, or community. See Lossky, *Orthodox Theology*.

5. See Harakas, *Toward the Transfigured Life*.

Part 5—Toward *Theosis*

the process and product of orienting everything in order to "seek first the kingdom" (Matt 6:33).

While some religions include an ascetic doctrine that the material world is bad or inherently evil, Christianity rejects such dualism (1 Tim 1:4–6). To the contrary, Christian asceticism seeks to redeem and reclaim the world and our desires: "Asceticism is the transfiguration of the eros and the passions and their redirection towards the divine, not their suppression or destruction."[6] Returning to our athletic metaphor, a runner that eats a specific diet during a training session has not necessarily dubbed other food bad, but as simply unprofitable during that time or for the goal at hand. Likewise, St. Paul tells us that although everything is good, not all things are profitable (1 Cor 9:12). Ascetic practices can redeem things like food and time by helping us to actually understand, appreciate, and contextualize these things in our lives and not be controlled by them. If I cannot control my impulses, then they control me, and I cannot submit my will to Christ. Asceticism is the process by which the Christian puts to death the passions (Col 3:5) and crucifies the flesh (Gal 5:24) in order to raise the body to life in the spirit. Therefore, by breaking the control of things over us we are made truly free in the spirit, and able to enjoy creation as it was meant for us.

As a concept, asceticism is more than just reaching goals. Asceticism is better understood as the purposed and reflective process of making the self, which all people do. That is, truly ascetic practices have as their goal or *telos* the changing of the self or community.[7] For the Christian, asceticism is a way to "achieve our authentic humanity" by uniting the self to Christ.[8] Properly understood, asceticism, although involving struggle, should invoke images of victory, freedom, growth, and personal and communal actualization.

---

6. Ware, forward to Yannaras, *Freedom of Morality*, 11.
7. For a discussion of this process, see Fagerberg, *On Liturgical Asceticism*.
8. Harakas, *Toward the Transfigured Life*, 32–39.

16

Why We Recite "Scripted" Prayers

Fr. Michael Bressem

OUR MODERN CULTURE LAUDS the freedom of "doing your own thing" or "just being yourself," so reciting scripted prayers in church may seem stifling or robotic. For some Christians, imagining themselves repeating the same litanies every Sunday is equivalent to requiring the congregation to wear uniforms and to march in orderly columns as they enter the sanctuary. Is the church a regiment of united souls lifting their voice in unison to petition their Creator? Or, is the church a loose community of individuals who uniquely express their needs to God as each person deems appropriate?

The debate over "scripted" (i.e., formal, composed) prayers versus "spontaneous" (i.e., casual, extemporaneous) prayers did not exist until the Protestant Reformation; prior to the sixteenth century, the church always saw the necessity for both, as both were taught or exemplified by our Lord (e.g., Matt 6:9–13; John 17). However, the Orthodox Church almost exclusively uses scripted litanies in her worship services.[1] Some Protestant denominations[2] judge the unvarying petitions of the Orthodox divine

---

1. Though not always done, the Orthodox liturgy allows the deacon (or the priest, if no deacon is present) to add spontaneous prayers to the litanies that address particular needs within the community, diocese, nation, or world. Also, many priests (or deacons or bishops) will offer a spontaneous prayer after the sermon.

2. Protestant denominations vary widely in their use of scripted prayers. "High church" Protestants, such as the Anglicans, will use scripted prayers during their services and often in their private devotions; whereas "low church" Protestants, such as those from the Brethren tradition, will rarely use scripted prayers (the Our Father being the only exception). Other denominations fall somewhere in the middle: they may occasionally use scripted prayers in their private devotions, but they will rarely use them during public church services.

liturgy to be verbose, impersonal, and suppressing of the Spirit. Why, then, do Orthodox believers recite scripted prayers?

Suppression or Inspiration?

The most assertive advocate for spontaneous prayer was John Bunyan.[3] His 1662 booklet *I Will Pray with the Spirit* passionately contended that prayer should be a "sincere pouring out of the soul to God." Bunyan inferred that it is not possible to sincerely recite scripted prayers (by that logic, one might ask whether our worship is insincere when we sing scripted hymns). He goes on to argue that prayer should be sensible, affectionate, assisted and strengthened by the Holy Spirit, and said in an attitude of submission to God for the good of the church. To all of this the Orthodox Church would say, "Amen."

Bunyan uses Romans 8:26 as his chief indictment against scripted prayer: "Likewise the Spirit also helps in our weaknesses. For we do not know what we should pray for as we ought, but the Spirit Himself makes intercession for us with groanings which cannot be uttered."

He asserts that we are ignorant of "what we should pray for" *only* when we pray spontaneously—inferring that the Holy Spirit is not making intercession when we recite scripted prayers. However, our spontaneous prayers can be just as contrary to what we ought to be praying for, as our hearts and minds can deceive us (Jer 17:9; 1 Cor 3:8–20); whereas traditional scripted prayers provide some assurance of being "tried and true": historically effective in eliciting spiritual benefit and in keeping with sound doctrine. Such cannot always be said when we are praying extemporaneously.[4]

Bunyan continues his treatise with a lengthy diatribe—addressing his reader as "thou poor, blind, ignorant sot"—against scripted prayer:

---

3. John Bunyan was of the Puritan denomination of Protestantism. He was most famously known for his Christian allegory, *Pilgrim's Progress*.

4. Oftentimes, when listening to someone who is praying extemporaneously, we are not prayerfully uniting our minds and heart with the person speaking; rather, we are often distracted with thoughts of figuring out what point the person praying is making and whether it is of sound Christian doctrine. Also, we are sometimes irritated that the person praying out loud is taking so long, may be pridefully trying to impress his listeners with his Christian jargon, or his words lack fluency. In sum, spontaneous prayers offered corporately often draw our attention more to the speaker than to God. Additionally, the one praying spontaneously can be so self-conscious of whether he is praying correctly, so as to not embarrass himself, that he is not attentive to the presence of God.

> This is the doom of those who do openly blaspheme the Holy Ghost, in a way of disdain and reproach to its office and service: so also it is sad for you, who resist the Spirit of prayer, by a form of man's inventing. A very juggle of the devil, that the traditions of men should be of better esteem, and more to be owned than the Spirit of prayer.

According to Bunyan, scripted prayers are the unforgiveable sin (Mark 3:29; Luke 12:10) and a work of the devil![5] Though most contemporary Protestants would hopefully not use such inflammatory rhetoric, some will argue that reciting scripted prayers "quenches the Spirit" (see 1 Thess 5:19).[6] They contend that we are suppressing the Holy Spirit's work within us when we recite scripted prayers. There are three problems with this position.

First, to believe a creature has the power to suppress the actions of an omnipotent Creator (e.g., Job 42:2; Matt 19:26) severely stretches the limits of credulity. Christ promised the Holy Spirit to work in our lives as a "Helper" (John 14:16; 15:26), Who will "guide [us] into all truth" (John 16:13). Therefore, how could the Holy Spirit, Whom the baptized Christian has received (Acts 2:38), not *help* or *guide* him to pray *unto all truth*?

Second, while it is possible to "resist" the Holy Spirit (see Acts 7:51), this is always a *conscious* act of disobedience, and nowhere in Scripture is reciting scripted prayers condemned as a sin. Last, those advocating for spontaneous prayer are arguably at greater risk of suppressing the Holy Spirit because they limit God's work of inspiration only to moments when people pray extemporaneously. The Holy Spirit "blows where it wishes" (John 3:8): the Holy Spirit can inspire people to write Scripture (2 Tim 3:16), to build tabernacles (Exod 35:30–31), to have visions (Rev 1:10), and to equip people to fulfill any godly ministry (1 Cor 12; Eph 4:1–13)—including writing prayers.

---

5. To be fair, Bunyan may have been directing his rebuke to the believer who only recites, or who consistently prefers, scripted prayers. However, the thesis of his treatise was that spontaneous prayers are superior to scripted prayers, and his arguments question whether scripted prayers are necessary at all. He acknowledges neither any benefits to scripted prayers, nor any drawbacks to spontaneous prayers. To this day, Protestant denominations that have their origins in the Puritan tradition (such as the Congregationalist Church), do not typically use scripted prayers in public services or in private devotions.

6. Actually, St. Paul mentions prayer two verses prior, and Bible commentators tend not to hold to this interpretation.

Part 5 — Toward *Theosis*

Verbosity or Beauty?

Another criticism frequently made against the use of scripted prayers is that they are perceived as being verbose and pompous. This position rests on two points. First, Jesus said: "When you pray, do not use vain repetitions as the heathen do. For they think that they will be heard for their many words" (Matt 6:7). However, the Greek transliteration of "vain," *battalogisitai*, which is more appropriately rendered as "babbling or prattling," refers to talking in an inarticulate or incoherent manner—just "empty phrases" (Matt 6:7 NRSV). But the litanies of the Orthodox Church are hardly meaningless.[7]

Scripture, itself, testifies to the use of scripted prayers. It is traditional for Jews to repeat the *Shema* at least twice a day (Deut 6:4–9). Jesus, himself, repeats his prayer three times in the garden of Gethsemene (Matt 26:36–44). Let us also not forget the four living creatures who "do not rest day or night, saying: 'Holy, holy, holy, Lord God Almighty, Who was and is and is to come'" (Rev 4:8; also Isa 6:3).[8]

The second point brought up by advocates of spontaneous prayer is that we should pray like a child to his father, using plain and simple language. Jesus stated: "Assuredly, I say to you, unless you are converted and become as little children, you will by no means enter the kingdom of heaven" (Matt 18:3).[9] However, Christ stated directly what he meant in

---

7. Note that Jesus was using as his example the "heathen" (also translated as "pagans" or "gentiles") in Matthew 6:7. Though we do not exactly know what religious practice Jesus was specifically referring to, it is not unusual for participants in some religious ceremonies to make all sorts incomprehensible ecstatic utterances, often while in a trance state, to beseech favor from their god. It is likely that Jesus was making a statement against rituals devoid of any meaning performed by people disobedient to God's commandments (as in Isa 1:10–15).

8. Other examples of repeated prayers: the New Testament Magnificat of Mary (Luke 1:46–55) and the Benedictus of Zechariah (Luke 1:67–79) bear resemblance to the Old Testament prayer of Hannah (1 Sam 2:1–10). The Lord gave us the parable of the tenacious widow (Luke 18:1–7) as encouragement "to pray and not lose heart" because God will respond to "His own elect who cry out day and night to Him." The *Didache* (also known as the *The Teaching of the Twelve Apostles*) was a late first or early second-century Christian treatise that covered various church practices. In section 8, it instructs believers to pray the Our Father three times a day. "Didache," 194.

9. The spontaneous prayer advocates also remind us that Peter and John "were uneducated and untrained men" (Acts 4:13), yet God answered their prayers in miraculous ways. And, reciting grand, elaborately scripted-prayers is viewed as not preserving the early church's quality of having "simplicity of heart" (Acts 2:46), and the Lord protects the simple-hearted (Ps 116:6). However, St. Paul was very educated, by contrast, and his

the following verse: "Therefore whoever humbles himself as this little child is the greatest in the kingdom of heaven" (Matt 18:4). His point was humility, not praying simply or plainly.

Consider that one of the attributes of God is beauty (Ps 45:2, 3), which is reflected in his creation (Eccl 3:11; Rom 1:20). Nature is both unique and repetitive, simple and complex. Therefore, it stands to reason that the prayers of his creatures would be both, as well. The prayers in the divine liturgy reflect the beauty that is found in the Psalms—many of which were scripted prayers.[10] Throughout Scripture, prayers are frequently neither brief nor plain, but rather eloquent and poignant. Examples include Daniel's prayer on behalf of the captive Jews (Dan 9:4–19) and Habakkuk's prayer for God to renew his miraculous deeds among his people (Hab 3).

Impersonal or Transpersonal?

Some spontaneous prayer advocates will contend that it is presumptuous to believe that an individual's scripted prayers can completely represent the unique and varied needs of others. Similarly, no prayer recited by us that was scripted by another is going to express everything within our hearts. There are three responses to this charge.

First, this position begs the question: why pray for others at all? We all tend to *guess* what will be of most benefit to others or ourselves when we pray—this is why we need the intercession of the Holy Spirit (Rom 8:26, 27). Nevertheless, we are admonished to seek the intercession of others and to pray for one another (Jas 5:13–18; see also 1 Tim 2:1). Our prayers, whether spontaneous or scripted, will likely fail to perfectly address the

---

prayers reflect this fact (e.g., Eph 1:15–23). That the early church was "simple-hearted" (Acts 2:46) speaks to the attitude of the early believers—being humble and charitable—rather than to their aptitude. In fact, Scripture speaks derisively of being "simple" of mind (Prov 1:22, 32; 7:7; 8:5; 9:4, 6, 16; 14:15, 18; 19:25; 21:11; 22:3; 27:12). Rather, God wants us to grow up and become mature in our understanding (1 Cor 2:6; Eph 4:13; Phlm 3:15; Col 4:12; Heb 5:11–6:3; Jam 1:4). Such maturity is likely to be reflected in our prayers, particular those which are carefully composed.

10. In Bibles that are translated from the Masoretic Old Testament—which is what Protestants commonly use—Psalm 72:20 (NIV) reads, "This concludes the prayers of David son of Jesse." It is likely that some psalms were composed extemporaneously (perhaps the brief and simple Psalm 134) whereas it is likely that other psalms were carefully crafted over a period of time (for instance, the long and complex Psalm 119 that follows an acrostic of the Hebrew alphabet).

Part 5—Toward *Theosis*

personal needs of others, but love compels us to intercede anyway (1 John 4).

Second, the ancient Jews had always used scripted prayers in their temple and synagogue worship services—the Psalms being an early collection of hymns and prayers written into books for their liturgies.[11] The early church, and the Orthodox Church to this day, patterned their worship after the Jewish liturgy—which was instituted and inspired by God in the Torah. There is no prohibition in the Bible, nor within the canons of the Ecumenical Councils, against the use of scripted prayers.

This second point is really the crux of the issue. Orthodoxy uses scripted prayers for their corporate worship because these prayers *unify* the faithful. There should be little doubt that the Bible values unity (e.g., 2 Chr 30:12; Ps 132:1; John 17:11, 20–23; Eph 4:1–5, 13; Col 2:2; 3:14, 15). One of the primary ways of preserving unity is for believers to pray together in unison, which is only possible if they are using scripted prayers in their services.[12] St. Paul desired for the church: "that you may with one mind and *one mouth* glorify the God and Father of our Lord Jesus Christ" (Rom 15:6, emphasis added).[13] Our corporate worship should be "transpersonal": beyond the interests of a single individual.

Third, scripted prayers were never meant to be "impersonal." While the congregation is attentive to the recited litanies, each individual adds petitions to the scripted prayers silently in their minds—thereby each person is giving their "personal touch."[14] Following the Holy Anaphora, the priest prays aloud for the bishops of the church, then the deacon adds: "Also remember, Lord, those whom each of us has in mind and all Your people." One of the values of scripted prayers, in both public and private devotions,

---

11. The Psalms seem to be divided into five books (Ps 1–41; 42–72; 73–89; 90–106; 107–50), and each book concluded with a doxology (41:13; 72:18–19; 89:52; 106:48; 150). This organization speaks to the likelihood that the books were intentionally used as liturgical references for Jewish worship. The Orthodox Church keeps to this tradition by reading from the Psalms during her services. There are many other parallels between the Orthodox divine liturgy and the Jewish liturgy.

12. St. Paul's instruction, "Let all things be done decently and in order" (1 Cor 14:40; see also 1 Cor 14:33), seems to preclude people saying spontaneous prayers aloud during a church service.

13. See also 1 Cor 1:10.

14. William S. Barker gives a well-reasoned argument from a Reformed Church perspective of a blending of the two forms of prayer. See Barker, "Prayers: Carefully Written or Spontaneous."

is that they prompt an individual to spontaneously pray over concerns that otherwise might not get addressed.[15]

In Whom Do We Trust?

During Divine service, during the celebration of all the sacraments and prayers, be trustful, as a child in relation to his parents. Remember what great Fathers of the Church, what inspired luminaries, enlightened by the Holy Ghost, are guiding you!

—St. John of Kronstadt

The debate over spontaneous and scripted prayers is not simply a difference of opinion regarding our interpretation of Scripture, but it is also a question of fidelity. Should we be "wise in [our] own eyes" (Prov 3:7; Isa 5:21) and so *only* trust ourselves by spontaneously praying? Rather, we should "ask for the ancient paths, ask where the good way is" (Jer 6:16 NIV), and therefore trust the scripted prayers of the two millennia-old Orthodox Church.

---

15. Scripted prayers also remind us of who God is, how to reverently address him, and what God wills for us. We often get so selfishly engrossed in spewing our own needs that we forget that we stand before the King of the Universe.

17

Are We Violating the Second Commandment? The Orthodox Teaching on Icons

Robert Arakaki

Upon their first visit to an Orthodox church, many Protestants are surprised by what they see. Instead of long rows of pews, the pulpit up front, and bare walls all around, they see images of Christ and the Virgin Mary on the icon screen up in the front, and more images of the saints on the walls all around.

These images are what Orthodoxy refers to as "icons." Icons are a part of the ancient Orthodox tradition. It is believed that the Evangelist Luke painted the first icon of the Virgin Mary holding the Christ Child. Orthodoxy believes that icons are more than illustrations; icons are windows to heaven. Every Orthodox church all around the world has icons in its sanctuary.

People have all sorts of reactions to their first visit to an Orthodox church. Some may be intrigued by how different everything is in an Orthodox worship service, while others may be unnerved and scared finding themselves in such unfamiliar surroundings. One question Protestants often ask when they see icons in an Orthodox church is whether this constitutes a violation of the second commandment:

> You shall not make for yourself a carved image—any likeness of anything that is in heaven above, or that is in the earth beneath, or that is in the water under the earth. (Exod 20:4)

When an Orthodox Christian hears this question, the first thing they should do is agree with the Protestant that the Bible is the authoritative and divinely inspired Word of God, and that all Christians should seek to follow the teachings of Scripture. Then they should seek to show how icons are compatible with Scripture.

Reading Scripture in Context

When reading the Bible it is important to place a passage in its proper context. Thus, in order to understand the second commandment one should take into account the first commandment (Exod 20:2–3), where Yahweh tells the Israelites that it was he who delivered them from Egypt and that they were to have no other gods. Ancient Egypt was polytheistic; it had many gods. The Egyptians made statues and images of the sky god, the earth god, the god of the Nile River, the cat god, the crocodile god, and so on. This suggests that the second commandment is not so much a prohibition against any and all religious images, but against the pagan worship of the Egyptians. They were to worship only Yahweh. The second commandment makes sense in light of the fact that the Israelites were heading to the land of Canaan which, like Egypt, was polytheistic. In other words, the intent and purpose of the first two commandments were to guard the Israelites from external pagan worship. Throughout their history, the Israelites were vulnerable to religious syncretism, adopting the worship practices of their pagan neighbors. This can be seen in Isaiah's warning against the making of statues (Isa 44). The second commandment's prohibition makes sense in its appropriate context: the images and statues of *external* pagan religions are forbidden, but this does not preclude the use of images in the *internal* Israelite worship of Yahweh. This becomes clearer when we read the second commandment in the context of the book of Exodus.

Images in the Old Testament

Exodus can be seen as having two halves; the first half covers God rescuing the Israelites from the Egyptians, and the second half contains instruction about the tabernacle, the place of worship. The tabernacle was a tentlike structure. It had a fence made up of hanging curtains all around the perimeter. We read in Exodus 26:1 the following: "Moreover you shall make the tabernacle with ten curtains of fine woven linen and blue, purple, and scarlet thread; *with artistic designs of cherubim you shall weave them*" (emphasis added). A similar curtain with an image of the cherubim woven in was to be made for the entrance to the holy of holies (Exod 26:31). Here Moses is being commanded by God to make curtains with images of angelic beings on them. These images are God's idea for what a place for worship should look like. No bare walls here!

The Mosaic tabernacle had images all around its perimeter, as well as at the entrance to its most holy place. This is much like the Orthodox Church today; images on the walls all around, as well up front at the entrance to the altar. Thus, Moses' tabernacle prefigured today's Orthodox churches.

Where Moses' tabernacle was a portable tent for a pilgrim community on their way to the promised land, Solomon's temple was a permanent structure for a settled community at rest in the promised land. Solomon's temple was patterned after Moses' tabernacle. The basic architecture was retained with some elaboration. In place of curtains were cedar walls with carvings of cherubim, palm trees, and flowers (1 Kgs 6:31-32; see also 2 Chr 3). The entrance to the Holy of Holies consisted of two olive wood doors with carved cherubim on them (1 Kgs 6:31; see also 2 Chr 3).

At the end of the book of Ezekiel is a vision of the future temple. We read in Ezekiel 41:17–20 that the future temple would have images on its walls, both in the inner and outer sanctuary. What is even more striking is the little detail that the image of the cherubim would be that of a human face alongside that of a lion. Ezekiel's temple sounds a lot like an Orthodox church, which has human faces (depicted in icons) on its walls, as well as on the icon screen leading to the altar area.

In summary, when we look at the Old Testament chronologically, we find consistent biblical support for the use of images in the house of worship, from Moses' tabernacle to Ezekiel's future temple. Images were part of Jewish worship from its beginning. Recent archaeological findings showed that Jewish synagogues around the time of Christ had images on their walls.

We Have Seen Him and Touched Him

A major turning point in human history took place in the incarnation. The eternal Son of God came down from heaven and took on human nature from the Virgin Mary. This is what people nowadays call a "game changer."

The infinite omnipresent Creator became a baby confined to a virgin's womb. The invisible God became tangible and visible. As the apostle John wrote:

> That which was from the beginning, which we have heard, which we have *seen with our eyes*, which we have *looked upon*, and our hands have handled, concerning the Word of life. (1 John 1:1, emphases added)

John of Damascus, an eighth-century father of the church, commented on what the Incarnation meant for the second commandment:

> It is clearly a prohibition against representing the invisible God. But when you see Him who has no body become man for you, then you will *make representations* of His human aspect. When the Invisible, having clothed Himself in the flesh, becomes visible, then represent the likeness of Him who has appeared. When He who, having been the consubstantial Image of the Father, emptied Himself by taking the form of a servant, thus becoming bound in quantity and quality, having taken on the carnal image, then *paint* and *make visible* to everyone Him who desired to become visible.[1]

Icons in Christianity

When we put the pieces of the Bible together what we find is that images have been part of the worship tradition of both the Old and New Testaments. Icons were part of biblical history and continued into church history. Early Christian places of worship had images. The early catacombs in Rome and the early church at Dura Europos (in Syria) displayed images of Christ and the Virgin Mary on their walls. Then, in the eighth and ninth centuries, there was an attempt by some Christians to do away with images in churches. They cited the second commandment as justification for their opposition to icons. This came to be known as the iconoclastic controversy. A major church council was convened in AD 787, and the use of icons in churches was upheld. It became an accepted universal practice to have religious images in early Christian churches.

When the Protestant Reformation emerged in the 1500s, there was a variety of positions taken on religious images. Some Protestants were

---

1. Ouspensky, *Theology of the Icon*, 44.

strongly opposed to having images in churches, while other Protestants saw no problems with images. When Protestantism came to America, many saw religious images in church as a distraction, and thus disallowed images. Protestantism's tendency to focus on the here-and-now also resulted in many of its members not knowing their church history. Because of this, many Protestants are surprised at seeing images of Christ and the saints when they visit an Orthodox church. It is the job of their Orthodox friend to explain how icons are consistent with Scripture and very much part of the historic mainstream of Christianity.

If one wants to introduce seekers and doubters to Orthodoxy, one can say what Philip said to skeptical Nathaniel: *Come and see!* As "windows to heaven," the icon is an invitation to an encounter with the Mystery of God. Christian faith is more than an intellectual assent to a concept of God; it is the heart seeking union with God. As one stands before the icon of Christ in the candle-lit darkness of an Orthodox church, one can almost hear the words of Jesus: "Blessed are the pure in heart, for they shall see God" (Matt 5:8).

18

Love in Action: The Orthodox Teaching on Almsgiving

Fr. Kevin Gregory Long

AMONG MANY OF THE indictments leveled at Christians, the accusation of greed is particularly challenging and troubling. Today, Christian authors and televangelists have promoted a type of "Gospel of Success" where wealth and acquisition become the primary goals, running contrary to what is found in the Scriptures. The New Testament reminds us frequently about the struggle we all must face against bad habits or vices, especially a vice like greed.

In the Orthodox Church, there is a strong emphasis on asceticism, with fasting being the most obvious way that this asceticism is practiced. When fasting, there is an emphasis on abstaining from particular types of foods, particularly animal products. However, right alongside the dietary concerns of fasting is the importance of increasing one's love of their neighbor, which is particularly underscored in the practice of almsgiving.[1] In this brief chapter, we will look at the core instruction for almsgiving as it is found in the New Testament and the works of Christian writers of the early church. These guidelines and reflections can serve as a helpful alternative to the gospel of acquisition and financial gain that can diminish the significance of the love and concern for God and one's neighbor.

---

1. The Greek term for almsgiving is ἐλεημοσύνη (*eleēmosynē*) which, in addition to the act of giving alms, can mean compassion, mercy or pity.

Part 5—Toward *Theosis*

Almsgiving in the New Testament

There are many references to almsgiving in the New Testament. In the Sermon on the Mount, Jesus Christ teaches that those who follow him should "give to him who asks you, and from him who wants to borrow from you do not turn away" (Matt 5:42; cf. Luke 6:30). In the Gospel of St. Luke, Christ says to his disciples:

> Do not fear, little flock, for it is your Father's good pleasure to give you the kingdom. Sell what you have and give alms; provide yourselves money bags which do not grow old, a treasure in the heavens that does not fail, where no thief approaches nor moth destroys. For where your treasure is, there your heart will be also. (Luke 12:32–34, emphasis added)

This tripartite stress on selling possessions, giving to the poor and storing up treasure in heaven is also found in the story of the rich young ruler (cf. Luke 18:18–23; Matt 19:16–22). The young man, having lived a virtuous life in keeping all of the commandments, asks Christ what he is lacking in order to inherit eternal life. He is saddened to learn that in order to be perfect, he has to sell what he has, give to the poor (thereby storing up treasure in heaven), and then follow Christ. He departs unhappily because he has many possessions and Christ is basically expecting him to abandon his way of life, and show mercy and compassion on others. He learns that priority should be given to the needs of the poor, even before one's own necessities.

Almsgiving is the fruit of the love for God and neighbor that is the cornerstone of a true follower of Christ.[2] Christ also reminds us that our love, care, and compassion are not based on how we will be received by the subject of our efforts, but on the very fact that this is the way that God deals with all of us: without preference, prejudice, or concern for reciprocation (cf. Luke 6:32–36).

The emphasis on selling all that one has and giving it to the poor continued in the early church, as portrayed in Acts

> Now the multitude of those who believed were of one heart and one soul; neither did anyone say that any of the things he possessed was his own, but they had all things in common. And with

---

2. "'You shall love the Lord your God with all your heart, and with all your soul, with all your strength, and with all your mind,' and 'your neighbor as yourself'" (Luke 10:27).

great power the apostles gave witness to the resurrection of the Lord Jesus. And great grace was upon them all. Nor was there anyone among them who lacked; for all who were possessors of lands or houses sold them, and brought the proceeds of the things that were sold, and laid them at the apostles' feet; and they distributed to each as anyone had need. (Acts 4:32; 33–35)

In Acts 10, Cornelius is called a righteous man because of his generosity through almsgiving (cf. Acts 10:1—11:18). Tabitha is also known for her generosity and concern for those in need. Her death was so discouraging to the young Christian community of Joppa that St. Peter came to where she was and brought her back to life (Acts 9:36–42). The compassion that Cornelius and Tabitha had for others, shown through their almsgiving to the poor and to widows, made them leaders and inspirations in the church as it developed.[3]

St. Paul in his Epistles also echoes the importance of caring for the poor through the giving of alms:

> Having then gifts differing according to the grace that is given to us, let us use them: if prophecy, let us prophesy in proportion to our faith; or ministry, let us use it in our ministering; he who teaches, in teaching; he who exhorts, in exhortation; he who gives, with liberality; he who leads, with diligence; he who shows mercy, with cheerfulness. (Rom 12:6–8)

Elsewhere, in 2 Corinthians, St. Paul continues this idea of taking each person's needs into account so that "now at this time your abundance may supply their lack, that their abundance also may supply your lack—that there may be equality" (2 Cor 8:14; see 2 Cor 8: 1–15 for the whole context).

The teachings of Jesus Christ, as well as the focus of the apostles as found in Acts and in the Letters of Saint Paul, all keep this stress on almsgiving as a key element to the practice of the Christian faith. This emphasis continued well into the time of the rise of the Byzantine Empire.

Almsgiving in the Early Church

During the fourth and fifth centuries, the church faced many challenges. One of these challenges was the increasing dilution of the core practices

---

3. On the contrary, there are also examples of people who hoarded money or had the wrong approach to how the church worked with respect to alms. See the stories of Ananias and Sapphira (Acts 5:1–10) and Simon the former magician (cf. Acts 8:14–23).

of the community.[4] This dilution took many different forms, but one of the most notable to figures like Saint John Chrysostom,[5] Saint Basil the Great,[6] and Saint Gregory of Nyssa[7] was the lack of almsgiving in the church. All three of these saints (along with others) wrote many letters, sermons and treatises concerning the practice of almsgiving and the notable lack of charity among the people in the church. They exhorted their parishioners to maintain the course of their practice of fasting with particular emphasis on the giving of alms.

Saint John Chrysostom speaks at length about a couple of key vices that are remedied by the practice of almsgiving. The vice of greed can cause a person to believe that material things are of greater worth than people. Almsgiving helps to reorient the giver into recognizing that all things, earned or otherwise, are gifts from God. As such, there are no real possessors of things, and there are certainly no entitlements to things that some people are more worthy of than others. Loving God completely means loving the neighbor completely: sharing one's own assets and making sure that no one else is in need. Almsgiving is the antidote to selfishness, serving to liberate people from an overly materialist and self-centered world view.

Likewise, giving alms—when done properly—helps to create an awareness of just who one's neighbor is: everyone. Vices of self-interest and pride are diminished when alms are given to everybody, without preferential treatment, without concern for how the alms are received, or without care or concern for what kind of acclaim will be received when the gift is given. Giving in this way increases the love that a person has for other people. It increases the humility in a person because it gives them an awareness of the people—and the needs of those people—around him or her.

> But you say, "I am poor." Even so, give what you have. God does not seek that which is beyond your strength. Give your bread; to one, give a drink of wine and to another, a garment. In this way the charity of many dissolves the misfortune of one person . . . Do you not see that the offering of the widow surpasses the one from the rich man? She gave everything in her possession (Mark 12:42).[8]

4. See Saint John Chrysostom's sharply critical comments concerning the priorities of the people of Antioch in his First Sermon on Lazarus and the Rich Man. St. John Chrysostom, *On Wealth and Poverty*, 19.

5. Ibid.

6. Basil, *On Social Justice*.

7. Gregory of Nyssa, *Concerning Almsgiving*.

8. Gregory of Nyssa, *Concerning Almsgiving*.

From these church fathers we see that almsgiving is a way of life, a way of quelling the passion of greed. Making this a crucial part of a person's fasting period thus sets their focus properly: on God first and foremost, then neighbor, and then self.

Living a life in Christ means, as it says in the Scriptures, picking up your cross and following him. In the Orthodox Church, a discipline of fasting and almsgiving helps to set the focus properly on love of God and love of neighbor as oneself, amplifying virtues of humility, compassion and charity, and helping to diminish the passionate vice of greed.

19

The Orthodox View on Infant Baptism

Fr. Josiah Trenham

THE GREAT MYSTERY OF holy baptism works numerous miracles mentioned in the text of the Orthodox liturgical rite. These miracles include adoption, remission of sin, new birth, definitive union with Christ, and many more. Heeding her Head's teaching that to children belong the kingdom of God, the church bequeaths her great mysteries of baptism, chrismation and eucharist to the children of believers.

In the vast sweep of Christian history, the baptism of infants has been uncontroversial. Orthodox Christians practice it. Roman Catholic Christians practice it. The Protestant Reformers practiced it. How, then, did the baptism of infants become controversial in America, and why does it remain so in some evangelical traditions?

The United States has been profoundly shaped by an individualistic, Protestant culture. Yet even our American Protestant forebears, who settled this country, practiced infant baptism almost universally. However, over the course of the last two centuries America has been deeply influenced by Anabaptist theology and culture. That strain of the sixteenth-century Reformation, known to history as the Anabaptist movement, has experienced its most vital flowering in America over the course of the last two hundred years.

The Orthodox theology and practice of infant baptism strikes at the heart of the Baptistic milieu and American individualism. Central to this reform movement is the belief that infants should *not* be baptized, and that a pre-condition for baptism is that the candidate be mentally mature "enough" (there is no consensus on what exact age that is) to make a reasonable and conscious decision for himself. The Orthodox Church solidly rejects these beliefs.

The Biblical Basis of Infant Baptism

The Structure of God's Covenants

The Scriptures of the church teach the propriety of infant baptism. God appeared to Abraham while he was living in Ur of the Chaldeans (Babylonians), and told Abraham to set out on a journey. God Almighty promised to Abraham to be his God, and promised that Abraham and his descendants would be God's people. God entered into a covenant with Abraham, and gave to Abraham a sign and seal of their relationship. It was a divine stamp of ownership, a reminder that the possessor of the sign belonged to God. That sign was circumcision (Gen 17, Rom 4:11).

By circumcision God formally established his covenant relationship with Abraham and his seed:

> This is My covenant which you shall keep, between Me and you and your descendants after you: Every male child among you shall be circumcised; and you shall be circumcised in the flesh of your foreskins, and it shall be a sign of the covenant between Me and you. (Gen 17:10–11)

Through this physical and tangible sign one would know that he was in covenant with God. How would you have known if you were God's if you lived at the time? How would you know if you belonged to the Old Testament church? Your circumcision revealed this, for circumcision was the sign of membership.

Women were not circumcised in the Old Testament in order that they might serve as a sign pointing forward to the coming of Jesus. Israel learned through not being able to circumcise women that the bride could not provide the blood of redemption for herself. She needed a bridegroom. The bridegroom's blood was necessary. For the church today our bridegroom is Christ (Exod 4:24–26; Eph 5:22–33). He provided the redemption that we could not provide for ourselves. It was his blood that was shed on our behalf, and that we drink for our nourishment (Matt 26:28).

Let me share with you why this is all so important. St. Paul tells us that, today, circumcision has been done away with as the sign of the covenant. "For in Christ Jesus neither circumcision nor uncircumcision avails anything, but a new creation" (Gal 6:15). God no longer employs circumcision like he used to. Yet God has not changed the way he deals with people. He is still the God of the covenant. The covenant with Abraham has come to fulfillment in the New Covenant (Gal 3–4). God still uses physical means to communicate himself and his grace. He still employs a sign to distinguish his people from the world, and to mark them as his own. Today in the church of Jesus Christ that physical conveyor and sign is holy baptism. Baptism has replaced circumcision.

Hear St. Paul: "In Him you were also circumcised with the circumcision made without hands, by putting off the body of the sins of the flesh, by the circumcision of Christ, buried with Him in baptism, in which you also were raised with Him through faith in the working of God, who raised Him from the dead" (Col 2:11–12). St. Paul says that Christian believers have, in baptism, the fulfillment of circumcision. What circumcision was to Abraham and his descendants until the coming of the Christ in the flesh, baptism is to Christians. It is the mark of God's ownership and of our salvation (Rom 4:11).

Who should receive this covenant seal? God made it very clear who should receive this Old Testament sacrament. Listen to Moses once again, continuing where we left off previously: "He who is eight days old among you shall be circumcised, every male child in your generations, he who is born in your house or bought with money from any foreigner who is not your descendant" (Gen 17:12). Who was to receive the sign of God's covenant? Who was to be reckoned as God's people? Eight day old children of Abraham! Thus Abraham circumcised Isaac, and Isaac Jacob, and Jacob Joseph and his brothers, etc.

Infant circumcision is the biblical precedent for infant baptism. Circumcision was given to the infants of one or more believing parents, and the same is true today of baptism. Indeed, as St. Peter said on the day of Pentecost about the forgiveness God promises in baptism, "For the promise is to you and to your children, and to all who are afar off, as many as the Lord our God will call" (Acts 2:39). No criticism laid against infant baptism today could not be equally applied to infant circumcision.

The New Testament Oikos Formula

The second major line of biblical teaching which makes plain the divine origin of infant baptism is the "*oikos* formula." *Oikos* is the New Testament

Greek word for "household." *Oikos* is employed in a phrase that runs throughout the Old Testament and right through the New Testament.

Grasping this *oikos* formula allows us to clearly and concisely answer the question of whether baptism was administered in the New Testament according to the Abrahamic household model, or according to the modern Anabaptist model which emphasizes baptism as an individual and adult decision.

Repeatedly throughout the New Testament we come across incidents in which whole households were saved and baptized. So common is it that there is a clearly repeated formula about the "whole house" being saved or baptized. This is the *oikos* formula.

> And Jesus said to him, "Today salvation has come to this house, because he, too, is a son of Abraham." (Luke 19:9)

This is found in the story about Zaccheus, the tax gatherer. No other member of Zaccheus's family is mentioned in the story, yet Jesus does not say that salvation had come to just Zaccheus for his repentance, but that salvation had come to Zaccheus's household. The salvation of the household is the usual New Testament pattern, not the salvation of individuals (John 4:53; Acts 10:2; Acts 11:14, Heb 11:7–9; Matt 10:12–14). This household formula is exceptionally conspicuous in its relationship to baptism. The New Testament shows us that baptism is anything but an individual and adult decision. It was often a household decision which included infants who had no say in the matter. In baptism the solidarity of the family is the decisive consideration.

> Yes, I also baptized the household of Stephanas. Besides, I do not know whether I baptized any other. (1 Cor 1:16)

> "Sirs, what must I do to be saved?" So they said, "Believe on the Lord Jesus Christ, and you will be saved, you and your household." Then they spoke the word of the Lord to him and to all who were in his house. And he took them the same hour of the night and washed their stripes. And immediately he and all his family were baptized. (Acts 16:30–33)

These references to receiving the covenant sign of baptism are couched in the exact same language as the references to Abraham's reception of the covenant sign of circumcision. The Old Testament pattern of giving God's salvation and the sign thereof to the whole household, including infants like eight-day-old Isaac, carries right over into the New Testament. As a matter of fact, there is not one reference in the New Testament to any person being baptized who had been raised in a Christian home, and had finally become an adult and "able" to believe and be baptized. It simply did not happen. Infants were baptized together with the whole household, and those infants who were born into a Christian family were given the grace of baptism as infants after the pattern of Abraham.

The Historical Practice of Infant Baptism

The testimony of church history is clear that infants were consistently baptized. This is evident from the witness of the church fathers,[1] from the existence of liturgical services for the churching and baptism of infants, and from the nonexistence of liturgical texts specifying that the candidate must be an adult. While at some times and places in the first four centuries of the church, Christians sought to put off baptism—since they hoped to be baptized just prior to death—this practice was eradicated by the great church fathers of the fourth century.

The testimony of church history confirms the propriety of infant baptism, and should assure us that our practice is the furtherance of a fine and rooted legacy. We are its present guardians. It is no small responsibility. We should not forget that God nearly killed Moses because he was slack and had not circumcised his son (Exod 4:24–26). God takes the baptism of the infants of his adult children seriously.

Infant baptism is a testimony to God's grace preceding our actions. For it is he who condescends and bestows his generous love bountifully upon our seed before ever they can return thanks or express their love to him. It is an ever-living testimony to God's rich provision for our every need, including that which is our greatest need as newborn babes—to be born again into spiritual life, to be united to the Lord Jesus Christ, and to have our sins washed away into the depths of the ocean of God's love, never to be seen again.

---

1. E.g., see Origen, *Homilies on Leviticus*, 8.3.11; Augustine, *Literal Interpretation of Genesis*, 10.23.39; Cyprian, *Letters*, 64.2.5; Irenaeus, *Against Heresies*, 2.22.4; and John Chrysostom, *Baptismal Instructions*, 3.6.

20

The Eucharist Is Life

Paraskevè (Eve) Tibbs

OVER THE YEARS, I have had the honor of teaching many faithful theology graduate students, the majority of whom have been evangelical Protestant Christians. I remember distinctly one class-wide discussion in a systematic theology course about the practice of the eucharist in each of the diverse Christian traditions represented by the students in the course. One student shared that she and members of her Emergent Christian fellowship spontaneously "did communion" around a bonfire at the beach with Sun Chips and Dr. Pepper. Their spur-of-the-moment act of eating chips and soda together in the Lord's name represented for them an authentic symbolic commemoration of the Lord's Supper—"do this in remembrance of me" (Luke 22:19)—in view of the participants' personal embrace of the gospel message, and their intention to "do communion." However memorable it was for the participants, it stands in stark contrast to the eucharist of the early church and the Orthodox Church today. Disregarding for the moment that the biblical Lord's Supper was bread and wine, this version of "doing communion" needed no officiant, no unity of faith, no previous sacramental action (such as baptism), no preparation of the elements in advance, and no personal preparation by the participants (such as prayer, fasting, or repentance). It was an entirely symbolic human action, during which neither the elements nor the participants were expected to be transformed. What follows is a brief sketch of a few of the theological themes just mentioned, which highlight the profound importance of the eucharist at the center of the life and witness of the Orthodox Christian Faith.

Part 5—Toward *Theosis*

Entrance into the Heavenly Kingdom

One of the most-notable differences between the Orthodox eucharist and the worship of many other Christian traditions is that the Orthodox liturgy is not a solely-human action directed toward God, but is considered to be "heaven on earth" since Emmanuel ("God is with us") comes to us.[1] The opening words of the divine liturgy[2] in which the eucharist is celebrated—"Blessed is the kingdom of the Father and of the Son and of the Holy Spirit"—attest to the understanding that the earthly and human are entering the eternal kingdom of Jesus Christ.

One of the earliest glimpses into the liturgical practices of the primitive Christian church may be found in the *Didache*[3] (or "Teaching of the Twelve"), possibly written as early as AD 50. It describes the early church's understanding of the eucharist as a gathering into Christ's eternal kingdom: "Even as this broken bread was scattered over the hills, and was gathered together and became one, so let Your church be gathered together from the ends of the earth into Your kingdom."[4]

The earliest writings of the church also show us that then, as now in the Orthodox Church, the holiness of the action required special preparation and designated officiants.[5] Only a bishop (*episkopos*) (Acts 20:12) or a presbyter (*presvyteros*),[6] as the bishop's representative, is the instrument used by the Holy Spirit to consecrate the eucharistic offering. However, after consecration the eucharist may be offered to the faithful by a deacon (*diakonos*). Ultimately, however, the Orthodox understand that it is Christ himself, the high priest (Heb. 2:17; 4:14), who is the officiant at his eternal eucharist,[7] in which the earthly divine liturgy participates.

---

1. Schmemann, *Eucharist*, 20.

2. The two primarily liturgies of the Byzantine Orthodox are the divine liturgies of Saint John Chrysostom and Saint Basil the Great, the core of each of which had been established by the late fourth or early fifth century.

3. For an excellent review of the dating of the *Didache*, see O'Laughlin, *Didache*. Recent scholarship suggests that it may have been written as early as AD 50, but not later than AD 70.

4. "Didache," 194–95. Note also the prohibition (two lines down) against eating and drinking of the eucharist unless one has been baptized in the name of the Lord.

5. See Staniforth, *Early Christian Writings*.

6. The Letters to Timothy and Titus use these terms interchangeably, so that *episkopos/presvyteros* refers to the leader of the congregation, as well as the overseer/celebrant of the eucharist.

7. The concept of "eternal eucharist" collapses eschatology with ecclesiology. The

Created to Be Eucharistic

The word eucharist (*eucharistia*), literally means "giving of thanks" and it underscores a crucial understanding of what it means to have been created in the image, according to the likeness of God (Gen 1:26; 27). Metropolitan Kallistos Ware has reminded us that unlike other creatures, we humans can consciously and deliberately thank and praise God for everything he has done to make and save the world. We are not only able to live in the world, use it, and think about it, but we are also capable of seeing the entire world as a sacrament of God's presence, and therefore a means of communion with him. Therefore, we have been created as "eucharistic" beings, to offer the gifts of creation back to God in worship and thanksgiving.[8]

At the divine liturgy, we give back to God as an offering (*prosphora*), that which he has given us in the first place: "offering to You these gifts from Your own gifts, in all and for all."[9] The divine liturgy includes the preparation in advance of the elements being brought as an offering of thanksgiving.

Notably, the offered elements are always bread and wine,[10] in imitation of Jesus' example. The offerings are not brought in their "raw" form, however. Rather, it is bread, not sheaves of wheat; wine, not grapes that are brought to the altar. They have been transformed by human work and creativity as a true offering of our God-given talents back to God.[11] Similarly, St. Irenaeus, Bishop of Lyons, writing in the second century, emphasized the human contribution in the offering, which thereby enables even inanimate creation to participate in worship of its Creator:

> Just as the wood of the vine, planted in the earth, bore fruit in its own time, and the grain of wheat, falling into the earth and being decomposed, was raised up manifold by the Spirit of God who sustains all, then, by wisdom, they come to the use of human

---

marriage supper of the lamb, as described in Revelation 19: 6–9, is the timeless eucharist over which Christ, the high priest, presides. Its locus is the eternal kingdom of God in which the earthly bride of Christ (the church) participates through the divine liturgy.

8. Ware, *Orthodox Way*, 70.

9. From the consecration prayers of *The Divine Liturgy of St. John Chrysostom*.

10. Elements other than bread and wine are used only in extraordinary circumstances. E.g., Fr. Arseny, a priest imprisoned in the Soviet gulag, secretly celebrated the eucharist in the prisoners' barracks, consecrating the sparse offering of breadcrumbs and water offered by other prisoners. Alexander, *Father Arseny, 1893–1973*.

11. Ware, *Orthodox Way*, 70.

PART 5—TOWARD *THEOSIS*

beings and, receiving the Word of God, become Eucharist, which is the Body and Blood of Christ.[12]

In addition to the human preparation of the elements to be consecrated, the holy eucharist is reserved for those who have united themselves with Christ and his church by baptism (i.e., Holy Illumination) and the laying on of hands (i.e., chrismation). The eucharist is not understood as a "means toward unity" as it is in some non-Orthodox Christian traditions that practice "open communion." Rather, it is an expression and sign of the genuine unity of faith already existing by reason of common baptism into the body of Christ, and a shared belief with the historical church across all ages, and in every place.

Requiring baptismal unity for participation is as old as the church itself. St. Paul connects baptism and eucharist in his First Letter to the Church at Corinth (1 Cor 9–11). The first-century *Didache* clearly shows that the eucharist was always reserved only for those who had been baptized in the Lord's Name: "No one is to eat or drink of your Eucharist but those who have been baptized in the Name of the Lord."[13] Similarly, second-century saint Justin Martyr described the eucharistic practice of his day as requiring like belief, baptism into Christ's death and resurrection, and holy living:

> This food we call the Eucharist, of which no one is allowed to partake except one who believes that the things we teach are true, and has received the washing for forgiveness of sins and for rebirth, and who lives as Christ handed down to us.[14]

This Is My Body

Perhaps the most significant aspect of the Orthodox eucharist is that it is not a symbolic action or a memorial meal. The church then and now expected the descent of the Holy Spirit to transform the offered bread and wine into the holy body and blood of the Lord, Jesus Christ, taking seriously Christ's own words: "This is My body which is given for you; do this in remembrance of Me" *(Luke 22:19) and* "He who eats My flesh and drinks My blood abides in Me, and I in him" (John 6:56). The Orthodox

---

12. Quoted in Behr, *Irenaeus of Lyons*, 179.
13. "Didache," 195.
14. Justin Martyr, "First Apology," 286.

have never attempted to explain how this change takes place, however.[15] On this topic, Saint John of Damascus (seventh century) wrote:

> If you enquire how this happens, it is enough for you to learn that it was through the Holy Spirit . . . and we know nothing further save that the Word of God is true and energises and is omnipotent, but the manner of this cannot be searched out.[16]

The eucharist is mystery to be received as food and drink, yet not to be "seen" through physical eyes.[17]

All aspects of the rite are carried out with great reverence, respect, and even awe, and the faithful are called to "draw near" "with the fear of God, in faith and with love"[18] (1 Cor 11:27–29). As the body and blood of Jesus Christ, the holy eucharist is considered so sacred to the Orthodox communicant that no food or drink will be consumed for many hours prior to receiving the sacrament. The preparation before receiving the eucharist also typically includes a period of increased prayer, almsgiving, and fasting (usually consisting of abstaining from eating animal products and animal by-products) for a number of days, as well as regular participation in sacramental confession. Even during the rite, the Orthodox faithful take great care not to spill even a drop, and afterwards, will take care to neither inadvertently spit nor kiss with the holy eucharist still on one's lips. These practices may seem exaggerated to the non-Orthodox, but the eucharist is simply being treated as that which it is: the true body and blood of the crucified and risen Savior. Consider, once again, St. Justin Martyr:

> For we do not receive these things as common bread or common drink; but as Jesus Christ our Savior being incarnate by God's Word took flesh and blood for our salvation, so also we have been

---

15. There was a rather heated debate in the medieval West between Roman Catholics, who defined the change with the term "transubstantiation" using Aristotelian physics (the difference between the substance and accidents of a thing) to explain the transformation of bread and wine into body and blood, and Lutherans, who insisted upon the term "consubstantiation" to suggest a spiritual yet genuine presence of Christ in and around the elements of bread and wine (rather than a transformation of the actual elements). Although Metropolitan Ware notes that the term "transubstantiation" was used in the East in isolated instances, it was not used to explain what happened to the elements. Ware, *Orthodox Church*, 285.

16. John of Damascus, "Concerning the Holy and Immaculate Mysteries of the Lord," 738.

17. Meyendorff, *Byzantine Theology*, 204.

18. See the *Divine Liturgy of St. John Chrysostom*.

taught that the food consecrated by the Word of prayer which comes from him, from which our flesh and blood are nourished by transformation, is the flesh and blood of that incarnate Jesus.[19]

For the early church, however, the real question was not what happens to the elements, but what happens to the participants in the eucharist? Through the eucharist, the individual members are formed collectively by the Holy Spirit into the one ecclesial body of Christ (1 Cor 10:17). In fact, a careful study of St. Paul's teaching on the eucharist in 1 Corinthians 11:18 reveals that "church" (*ekklesia*) is used in a dynamic sense: "when you come together as a church." In other words, the church becomes the church fully when it celebrates the eucharist at the divine liturgy, in a way that it is not at other times. In this sense, the eucharist should not be considered as something the church *does*, but rather what the church *is*, or rather what it is always in the process of becoming. This is an important distinction between the Orthodox eucharist and the view of Christian traditions that "do communion." Metropolitan John (Zizioulas) of Pergamon asserts that even referring to the eucharist as one of the sacraments is improper, since it makes the eucharist an object. Properly understood, the eucharist is *the* mode of life of the congregation. What the church receives at the eucharistic divine liturgy is not just holy things, not even the words or deeds of Christ, but rather the "person of Christ in its totality."[20]

The essence of the intimate relationship of believers with Christ and one another is described as "communion" (*koinonia*) which is mentioned over twenty times in the New Testament, and is fundamental to every aspect of Orthodox thought and life:

> The cup of blessing which we bless, is it not the communion of the blood of Christ? The bread which we break, is it not the communion of the body of Christ? For we, though many, are one bread and one body; for we all partake of that one bread. (1 Cor 10:16–17)

A helpful word picture of the close physical communion of believers in Christ through the eucharist was provided by St. Cyril of Alexandria in his fifth-century commentary on John 6:56:

> Just as if someone were to entwine two pieces of wax together and melt them with a fire, so that both are made one, so too through

---

19. Justin Martyr, "First Apology," 286.
20. Zizioulas, *Eucharistic Communion and the World*, 26.

participation in the Body of Christ and His Precious Blood, He is united in us and we too in Him.[21]

The eucharist is where all the dimensions of communion are found: God communicates himself in the eucharist, where human persons enter into communion with him; the participants of the sacrament enter into communion with one another, and creation as a whole (in the bread and the wine) enters through humanity into communion with God.[22]

Conclusion

In conclusion, the differences between the Orthodox understanding of the eucharist and that of most evangelical Protestant Christians are significant. The eucharist in the Orthodox Church is not a solely-human response to a divine command to "do this in remembrance of me" but is an event of human/divine communion and a momentary participation in Christ's eternal banquet in the here and now. In order to be a true offering in thanksgiving of both the gifts and of ourselves, there must be a human element of preparation. The bread and wine are prepared from grapes and wheat by the members of the congregation and brought to the sanctuary, as the people also prepare themselves. The officiant priest or bishop then prepares the offering for consecration, while praying for the entire church of the living and those departed from this life. In the divine liturgy, the Holy Spirit is called upon to first descend upon the assembled congregation to make the individual flawed members of the congregation into the perfect body of Christ—the church—and then to descend upon the gifts offered to make them the precious body and blood of Jesus Christ. In a sense, the faithful participants must "be" the body of Christ before receiving the body of Christ. Only those who have prepared through prayer, almsgiving, fasting, and repentance will approach the chalice "with fear of God, faith and love" to receive the holy mystery, recognizing that it is truly Christ's body and blood "for the forgiveness of sins and eternal life" (Matt 26:28; John 6:53–54). Simply put, the eucharist of Orthodox Christianity is not a symbolic human gesture, but is the locus of the most intimate (physical and spiritual) communion possible of the members of the church with Jesus

---

21. Cyril of Alexandra, *Commentary on John*, 223–24.
22. Zizioulas, *Being as Communion*, 81.

Christ himself. It is also a spiritual communion of the faithful with one another, brought together by the Holy Spirit in Christ as the body of Christ.

21

Why Must I Confess My Sins to a Priest?

Mother Melania

IF YOU HAVE EVER lived in another culture, you know that many customs make no sense until you start to think like a member of that culture. Likewise, many Orthodox customs seem strange to modern-day people because of fundamentally different presuppositions. As members of contemporary society, we are very individualistic. The Orthodox, however, having as a basic presupposition that we are the body of Christ, are fundamentally community oriented.

Thus, you may think, "If I do something wrong, that is between me, the person I wronged, and (maybe) God. Why involve a priest?" An Orthodox Christian, however, would consider it obvious that the malfunctioning of one member affects the entire body (cf. 1 Cor 12:24–26). Therefore, unresolved sin is a matter of concern to the whole church. In fact, in the first centuries, those who committed serious sins confessed before the entire congregation![1]

Scripture clearly reveals a public church discipline. For example, a person who has been wronged must go privately to the one who committed the wrong, then with another person, then to the whole community. If all of this fails, the one at fault is excluded from the community. The passage continues, "Assuredly, I say to you, whatever you bind on earth will be bound in heaven, and whatever you loose on earth will be loosed in heaven" (Matt 18:15–18). Here the power of binding and loosing (of sins) seems to be given to the entire church. For, while this power is given specifically to St.

---

1. Since sin was social and ecclesial, repentance was also social and public. Dallen, *Reconciling Community*, 36.

Peter[2] two chapters earlier (Matt 16:18–19), it is elsewhere (John 20:21–23) given to all the apostles. The following story illustrates how the power of "binding and loosing" lies in one sense with the apostles and in another sense with the whole church.

Aghast that a Corinthian Christian is openly living with his father's wife, St. Paul commands the Corinthian church to excommunicate him "when you are gathered together" (cf. 1 Cor 5:1–7). Later, he instructs the whole community to forgive and comfort the repentant sinner (cf. 2 Cor 2:5–8). So, the whole community was involved in restoring the person (i.e. binding and loosing), but did so in obedience to the apostle (later, to the bishops—the apostles' heirs).

Public penance was reserved for the most serious sins, such as murder, adultery, or apostasy (for everyday sins, the ongoing life of the church was sufficient remedy).[3] Eventually, the conditions of penance became so difficult that only the saintly were willing to undergo it.[4] This situation, combined with the monastic custom of spiritual direction,[5] gave rise to confession as we know it—confessing to God in the presence of a priest.[6]

These two strands highlight two major reasons for the sacrament of confession—(1) reconciliation with God and the church, and (2) help in *staying* reconciled. Confession is, first and foremost, the sacrament of reconciliation. For a member to be at odds with the head and the rest of the body is a matter of life and death. The member's sickness, left unattended, can affect the entire body and will eventually cause the member's death (cf.

---

2. The Orthodox have always understood the authority granted to St. Peter as extending to the other apostles and, eventually, their successors, the bishops. E.g., Blessed Theophylact says, "By keys, understand that which binds or looses transgressions, namely penance or absolution; for those, like Peter, who have been deemed worthy of the grace of the episcopate, have the authority to absolve or to bind . . . Even though the words 'I will give unto thee' were spoken to Peter alone, yet they were given to all the apostles." Stade, *Explanation by Blessed Theophylact*, 141.

3. "This formal procedure was required only in extraordinary cases. Ordinary sinners followed the path of repentance through the prayer, mortification, and good works that characterized the everyday life of Christians . . . In either situation, however, forgiveness of sins came through solidarity with the Church and through its prayer." Dallen, *Reconciling Community*, 42, 61.

4. Ibid., 76.

5. Ibid., 103–5.

6. Some Orthodox insist that we do not confess to a priest, but confess to God in the presence of a priest. (See, e.g., Shanbour, "Sacrament of Confession"). Thus, I have avoided saying, "We confess to a priest." However, as will be shown below, this is true in one sense, but not in another.

Melania—Why Must I Confess My Sins to a Priest?

1 Cor 5:1–7). We cannot restore this broken relationship ourselves—God must act. In the sacrament of confession, God reconciles us with himself and with the church, Christ's body. This is why confession is sometimes called "the baptism of tears" or "the second baptism." In baptism, we are washed in water and made new in Christ.[7] In confession, by God's grace, we are washed in our tears, forgiven and given a new start.

Still, this does not answer the question, "Why do I need a priest?" An anecdote may help. A Russian empress was visiting a village parish. When she tried to kiss the village priest's hand, he drew it back. The empress said, "I am kissing Christ's hand, not yours!" The empress correctly understood that she was kissing the hand of Christ, of whom the priest is an image. Yet, the hand was both Christ's and the priest's. So, she was, in fact, kissing the hand of Christ *and* the hand of the priest.

With this in mind, consider the following prayer recited by priests at the end of confession:

> My brother, inasmuch as thou hast come to God, and to me, be not ashamed; for thou speakest not unto me, but unto God . . . I, humble and a sinner, have not power on earth to forgive sins, but God alone; yet through that divinely spoken word which came to the Apostles . . . saying: Whosoever sins ye remit, they are remitted, and whosoever sins ye retain, they are retained, we too are emboldened to say: Whatsoever thou hast said to my most humble self . . . God forgive thee in this present world, and in that which is to come.[8]

The priest says, "Thou speakest not unto me, but unto God," but also, "Whatsoever thou hast said to my most humble self . . . may God forgive." Likewise, while the priest claims to have no power on earth to forgive sins, he acknowledges his share in the apostolic power of remitting and retaining sins. The apparent contradiction is resolved in the priest's being both himself and the image of Christ. In and of himself, the priest is like us—frail, sinful and in need of confession. So, in his own person, he has no power

---

7. "The sacrament of penance is our formal act of reconciliation with God in the Church when sin has severed us from the Church's life. Because penance is the way to communion with God when that communion has been broken by sin, it is often referred to in Church Tradition as the renewal of baptism, or as the reestablishment of that condition of life with God which was given to men in the basic sacraments of inauguration into the Christian life." Hopko, *Worship*.

8. *Pocket Prayer Book for Orthodox Christians*, 44–45.

to forgive sins, but as the image[9] and representative of Christ (and heir of the apostles), he does.[10] Further, since the priest is the image of Christ, the church's head, the sacrament involves the whole body of Christ and thus is still "public." So, through the priest, in the sacrament of confession, the member is restored to Christ's body, and Christ's body is restored to fullness. A mighty miracle indeed!

Still, just as medicine cannot permanently heal a person who lives an unhealthy lifestyle, so those whose hearts are filled with ungodly thoughts will keep succumbing to the same spiritual sicknesses. Thus, we come to the second great benefit of confession—it helps us to *stay* reconciled to Christ and his church. This is the function of "penances" (specific acts that the priest assigns in consequence of certain sins confessed)—from the long, painstaking penances of earlier centuries to today's comparatively light ones. They are not impersonal punishments, but remedies, and therefore may be lighter or heavier depending on the condition of the penitent's heart. Yet along with these penances, we must still realign our thoughts with those of Christ, or else we will fall into the same old patterns that caused us to estrange ourselves from Christ and each other in the first place—thus the need for the spiritual counsel aspect of confession.[11]

Maybe you are thinking, "That may make sense in its own context, but there is no way that I, a twenty-first-century American, am going to accept such a practice! Does not it make me a second-class citizen compared to the priest? What about my autonomy? And, frankly, it is horribly embarrassing!"

---

9. The understanding of the priest (or, more accurately, the bishop as the high priest) as the image of Christ was reached very early in church history. This famous passage was written during the first generation after the apostles: "And say I, Honour thou God indeed, as the Author and Lord of all things, but the bishop as the high priest, who bears the image of God—of God, inasmuch as he is a ruler, and of Christ, in his capacity of a priest." Ignatius, "Epistle to the Smyrneans," 233.

10. "What priests do on earth, God ratifies above. The Master confirms the decisions of his servants. Indeed, he has given them nothing less than the whole authority of heaven. For he says, 'Whoever's sins you forgive are forgiven, and whoever's sins you retain, they are retained.' What authority could be greater than that? 'The Father has given all judgment to the Son.' But I see that the Son has placed it all in their hands." Chrysostom, *Treatise concerning the Christian Priesthood*, 65.

11. Spiritual direction *per se* does not *require* a priest. An experienced monastic or even a wise layperson can provide excellent spiritual direction. However, the two parts of confession go together naturally—the priest who has heard my confession and who knows me is in a good position to offer advice for how not to repeat these same sins.

Melania—Why Must I Confess My Sins to a Priest?

To answer the first question, "No! While there is definitely hierarchy in the church, there are no second-class citizens." In Christ's body all members are needed and those who seem less honorable are to be given more honor and care (cf. 1 Cor 12:1–31). True, the priest has been given the power to remit and retain sins, but again, this is as Christ's image and representative, not in his own person. Any priest will tell you how greatly he respects those who honestly and deeply confess their sins, and how much help he gets in his own spiritual life from witnessing people courageously dealing with their own sins. So, here is another outworking of this basic law of the body of Christ—those who humbly confess receive honor from those to whom they confess!

As for autonomy, is there really such a thing? We are all dependent on a myriad of other people (not to mention animals, plants, and inanimate objects) for having been born at all and continuing to exist. Acknowledging this does not diminish our personhood, but enriches our lives and brings us joy. As this relates to confession, yes, I can confess directly to God and should do so as soon as I realize I have sinned. Yet I do not sin in a vacuum. My sin affects the rest of the body (and indeed the rest of creation) and I need the help of the entire body, but particularly the priest as the image and representative of Christ, to be restored.

As for embarrassment, yes, confession can be deeply embarrassing. Confession is, among other things, quite a lesson in humility. There is no true Christianity without humility, and getting there is extremely painful for most of us. At some level, though, we all understand the need to confess to another person (even if it is just our psychologist) and know the great relief that comes from doing so and finding acceptance and perhaps even help to overcome our fault. In thus opening ourselves up to another, we take a small step toward healing the division between us and the rest of mankind and all of creation. It is not easy, but well worth it. How much greater, then, are the healing and joy that come through sacramental confession as we are reconciled to Christ, his body, and all creation?

So, we confess to God in the presence of the priest—who is a human being like us but also the image and representative of Christ. In doing so, we are reconciled to Christ and to his body, so that we may be free to be who we in fact are—members of Christ.

PART 6

Our Friends in Christ

22

Why All the Focus on Mary? The Orthodox Teaching on the Theotokos

Fr. Steven Ritter

THERE HAS BEEN NO other woman in the history of the world so extoled in art, music, and literature as the Virgin Mary. From Da Vinci, Botticelli, Dali, and Rubens, to Mozart, Bach, Palestrina, and Stravinsky, her image has been embedded in the very seeds of Western Culture. John Calvin believed that "we cannot enjoy the blessing brought to us in Christ without thinking at the same time of that which God gave as adornment and honor to Mary, in willing her to be the mother of his only-begotten Son."[1] And, as Martin Luther stated, "She became the Mother of God, in which work so many and such great good things are bestowed on her as pass man's understanding."[2]

Yet for many Protestant Christians today, Mary is rarely given a second thought, save that which passes once a year during the Christmas season when the reading of the story of the birth of Christ takes place in church or in a family setting. Because of this exclusive familiarity with this one aspect of Mary's role it can seem difficult and even unreasonable to entertain the possibility of something deeper at work here.

Of all the creatures ever fashioned by the Creator, Mary, the *Theotokos* (or "Birth-giver of God"), stands out as the most perfect example of our humanity that has ever existed, one that we *venerate* without limit, even as we reserve our *worship* for God alone. One of the services of the Orthodox Church, at the time of the nativity celebrations, proclaims,

1. Calvin, *Harmony of Matthew, Mark and Luke*, 32.
2. Pelikan and Lehmann, *Luther's Works*, 326.

Part 6—Our Friends in Christ

> What shall we offer Thee, O Christ, who for our sakes hast appeared on earth as man? Every creature made by Thee offers Thee thanks. The angels offer Thee a hymn; the heavens a star; the Magi, gifts; the shepherds, their wonder; the earth, its cave; the wilderness, the manger: and we offer Thee a Virgin Mother. O pre-eternal God, have mercy upon us.[3]

The honor and veneration given to Mary begin precisely here: with *us*. For us to truly understand her role in the economy of salvation, her importance to the Christian faith, we must realize the dignity and exalted place of *mankind* in the Lord's eyes. As the pinnacle of creation, and highly-beloved in the sight of God, the human race, even in its "fallen" state is still able, because of the image of God residing in each human being, to respond to the love of *He Who Is,* the great "I AM" of the scriptures—Jesus Christ our Lord. "Before Abraham was, I AM" (John 8:58), Jesus exclaimed to the Pharisees, thereby equating himself with the great God of heaven. And this "I AM," when he chose to come and live among his creatures, could have none other than the most beauteous and perfect offering possible as the vehicle of his incarnation. Her name is Mary.

For Orthodox Christians, the very name itself is enough to inspire the most exalted of feelings. They take very seriously the appellation given to her in the New Testament, "highly favored" (Luke 1:28) or "blessed" (Luke 1:38). These words do not describe her simply because she was chosen to bear the God of the universe in her womb, though that is certainly reason enough; but also because her entire life was one of being "grace-filled" (*charitoo* in the original Greek). It all comes down to what we think of the notion of *holiness*. When something is "holy unto the Lord," it is set aside for sanctification, *and never returns to common use,* just as the apostle Paul cautions all of us who have put on Christ to avoid returning to the errors of our former lives. We are new creatures who are set aside, sanctified—"made holy." For Mary, being chosen to bear the Son of God makes her person the holiest vessel that the world has ever known. For this, she was chosen in the mind of God before the very creation of the universe. His foreknowledge conceded her free-will acceptance of the role, and she was carefully schooled in the ways of holiness and obedience to God even before the Archangel's announcement. "Let it be to me according to your word."[7] This is no response from a young girl chosen randomly or capriciously, but of

---

3. Mother Mary, *Festal Menaion,* 254.

a person touched her entire life by divine grace. "Everything we aspire to become in Christ, she already is."[4]

The Old Testament is replete with references to her whom all generations shall call blessed. Perhaps most properly, she is likened to the tabernacle that held God, the sanctuary of his glory, while the Israelites were wandering in the desert (Exod 25—27:19). Many today, in absolute concordance with the prophesy found in the book of Isaiah (Isa 7:14), claim to believe in the "virgin birth," but Orthodoxy insists on pressing the question—did Mary simply *conceive* while still a virgin, or did she indeed *give birth and remain* a virgin? The true miracle proclaimed by the very earliest teachers of the church is that the Lord has overturned nature (just as he will do in the general resurrection), with Mary's virginity—before, during, and after the delivery. It finds prominent scriptural support from the Prophet Ezekiel referring to the "east gate":

> Then He brought me back to the outer gate of the sanctuary which faces toward the east, but it was shut. And the Lord said to me, "This gate shall be shut; it shall not be opened, and no man shall enter by it, because the Lord God of Israel has entered by it; therefore it shall be shut. As for the prince, because he is the prince, he may sit in it to eat bread before the Lord; he shall enter by way of the vestibule of the gateway, and go out the same way." (Ezek 44:1–3)

Of course, there are those who also balk at the idea of Mary choosing to *always* remain a virgin after the birth of Jesus. "Why would she do this?" they ask. The answer lies in the important concept mentioned earlier, as we return to the idea of *holiness*. The Lord who said, "Be holy, for I am holy" (1 Pet 1:16), also uttered these words: "No one, having put his hand to the plow, and looking back, is fit for the kingdom of God" (Luke 9:62). Mary, chosen in the eyes of God before all the ages, agreed to accept the flesh of the immortal God in her womb. Because of this, the fact of holding the eternal God within herself, she became "more spacious than the heavens."[5] Her person has known God in the most intimate manner possible. How could she then, having given birth to God the Son in the flesh, return to the common lot of bearing children, as exalted a role as that is? It is not possible for her body, now sanctified and rendered holier than the ark of the covenant itself, to be returned to "everyday" use. Search the

---

4. Gillquist, *Becoming Orthodox*, 110.
5. *Prayer Book for Orthodox Christians*, 28.

Scriptures and you will find that holiness is not heralded in this way—once something is consecrated, it is *always* consecrated, and Mary was the first to realize this.

Mary's motherhood and virginity are *one* in the eyes of the Lord, perpetually. "Her sexuality was transformed into everlasting motherhood to God, and, inseparably, to everlasting virginity. She became the Mother of God, not for nine months, not for thirty-three years, but forever."[6] As such, in the carefully constructed relationship between us and God, her intercessory power is great. She whose role it is to say "whatever He [Jesus] says to you, do it" (John 2:5) now becomes *our* mother because she is the mother of Christ, whose body is the church (1 Cor 12).

Mary's place in the history of humanity is that of the greatest woman—and indeed, human being—who has ever lived, aside from our Lord Jesus Christ, who is God *and* man. She is the prototype of all *we* should be, and if we care about the biblical mandate that "all generations shall call me blessed" (Luke 1:48) then we must think about this seriously and begin to understand the reasons for this utterance. As she is the first among the saints, we praise the name *Theotokos* and thereby glorify the church, for without her "there is no Christ and no Church . . . all men are her children, Christians and non-Christians alike, because she mediated human life to God and divine life for all mankind."[7] Because of this extraordinary role, her intercession is profound, our greatest partner in prayer before God, who out of his overflowing love came to us in order to proclaim our salvation and rescue us from sin and death. Her honor is but an extension of *our* dignity as sons and daughters of God—she represents the very best of all of us, our offering to God, and is linked to him in a way that we can only begin to understand.

---

6. Gabriel, *Mary*, 42.
7. Ibid., 165.

23

The Communion of Saints

David C. Ford

THE APOSTLES' CREED, IN use in the Western church since the fourth century of the Christian era and still used by the Roman Catholic Church and some Protestant churches in regular worship services, contains the phrase, in a list of what Christians believe in, "the communion of saints." Historically, this phrase refers to the saints living with Christ in heaven, and the active fellowship with them which Christians experience while living on this earth. These saints are referred to by the apostle Paul as "the spirits of just men made perfect" in his description of Christian worship in Hebrews 12:22–23:

> But you have come to Mount Zion and to the city of the living God, the heavenly Jerusalem, to an innumerable company of angels, to the general assembly and church of the firstborn who are registered in heaven, to God the Judge of all, *to the spirits of just men made perfect.* (emphasis added)

Earlier in this same book, after mentioning some of the great deeds of many of the great Old Testament men and women of faith, Paul writes, "Therefore we also, since we are surrounded by *so great a cloud of witnesses*, let us lay aside every weight, and the sin which so easily ensnares us, and let us run with endurance the race that is set before us" (Heb 12:1, emphasis added).

"So great a cloud of witnesses"—these are the saints, both known and unknown, both officially canonized/glorified and not so officially recognized, who constantly surround us, accompanying us on our journey to the heavenly life of which they are already experiencing a foretaste. While their

Part 6—Our Friends in Christ

bodies are dead and buried, their spirits are alive and awake in Christ, for as Jesus said,

> But even Moses showed in the burning bush passage that the dead are raised, when he called the Lord "the God of Abraham, the God of Isaac, and the God of Jacob." For He is not the God of the dead but of the living, for all live to Him. (Luke 20:37–38)

We see the souls of the martyrs alive and awake in the book of Revelation:

> When He opened the fifth seal, I saw under the altar the souls of those who had been slain for the Word of God and for the testimony which they held. And they cried with a loud voice, saying, "How long, O Lord, holy and true, until You judge and avenge our blood on those who dwell on the earth?" (Rev 6:9–10)

And as Paul said, he yearned for his earthly life to be over so that he could be more completely in the Presence of the Living God: "For to me, to live is Christ, and to die is gain . . . For I am hard-pressed between the two, having a desire to depart and be with Christ, which is far better" (Phlm 1:21–23).

In addition, we find two examples of the Old Testament saints continuing to be alive and awake in the next life in the account of Christ's transfiguration on Mt. Tabor, when we see Moses and Elijah conversing with him (Luke 9:30–33).

The ineffable unity of the church on earth with the church in heaven is beautifully and powerfully described by St. John of Kronstadt, a widely known and very beloved married priest in Russia in the nineteenth and early twentieth centuries:

> God's Saints, as our brethren—but perfect—live, and are near us, ever ready to help us, by the grace of God. We live with them, in the house of our Heavenly Father, only in different parts of it. We live in the earthly, they in the heavenly half; but we can converse with them, and they with us.
>
> How closely the Church in Heaven and the Church on earth are connected! What love the Church has! She unceasingly remembers the Church in Heaven, She calls upon its members in prayer, and gives glory to them for the great deeds which they wrought upon earth for God's sake. She unceasingly prays for the whole body of the Church on earth, and intercedes for the departed, in

the hope of the resurrection unto life eternal, and of union with God and the Saints.

Let us enter into the spirit of this great love of our Mother the Orthodox Church; let us be penetrated with it. Let us look upon all our brethren—*both in Heaven and on earth*—as our own members, as *we are all members of the one body of the Church*, and let us love them actively, as we love ourselves. Then shall we be living members of the Church in Heaven, and She will be our active and speedy helper and intercessor.

We ought to have *the most lively spiritual union* with the dwellers in Heaven, the Apostles, Prophets, Martyrs, saintly bishops, confessors, with all the Saints, as they are all members of the one body, the Church of Christ, to which we sinners also belong, and the living Head of which is the Lord Jesus Christ Himself. This is why we call upon them in prayer, converse with them, thank and praise them. *It is urgently necessary for every Christian to be in union with them if he desires to make Christian progress*; for the Saints are our friends, our guides to salvation, who pray and intercede for us.[1]

We also notice in this passage St. John's emphasis on the role which the saints in heaven have in praying and interceding for us. Since they are alive and awake in Christ, and are filled with the grace of the Holy Spirit, they know through the Holy Spirit about our trials and tribulations. So we ask them to pray for us, just as we ask our friends and relatives here on earth to pray for us. We get a glimpse of the reality of the prayers of the saints described in the book of Revelation as part of the ongoing heavenly worship: "Then another angel, having a golden censor, came and stood at the altar. He was given much incense, that he should offer it with *the prayers of all the saints* upon the golden altar which was before the throne. And the smoke of the incense, *with the prayers of the saints*, ascended before God from the angel's hand" (Rev 8:3–4, emphasis added). And we could add that, since the saints are dwelling so close to Christ in the heavenly realm, we can most probably assume that their prayers will be even more effective than those of our loved ones on earth.

St. Silouan of Mt. Athos (1866–1938), talks about the communion of saints in these words:

---

1. Grisbrooke, *Spiritual Counsels of Father John of Kronstadt*, 63–64, emphasis added.

Part 6—Our Friends in Christ

> The Saints were people just like ourselves. Many of them started with grievous sins, but through repentance they attained the kingdom of Heaven . . .
>
> In the kingdom of heaven the holy saints look upon the glory of our Lord Jesus Christ; but through the Holy Spirit they see took the sufferings of men on earth. The Lord gave them such great grace that *they embrace the whole world with their love*. They see and know how we languish in affliction, how our hearts have withered within us, how despondency has fettered our souls, and they never cease to intercede for us with God.
>
> The Saints rejoice when we repent, and grieve when men forsake God and become like unto brute beasts . . .
>
> The Saints in Heaven through the Holy Spirit behold the glory of God and the beauty of the Lord's Countenance. But in this same Holy Spirit they see our lives too, and our deeds. They know our sorrows and hear our burning prayers. When they were living on earth they learned of the love of God from the Holy Spirit, and he who knows love on earth *takes it with him into eternal life in the Kingdom of Heaven*, where *loves grows and becomes perfect*. And if love makes one unable to forget a brother here, how much more must the Saints remember and pray for us![2]

This ineffable oneness of the saints in heaven with all of us Christians on earth, who are "called to be saints" (Rom 1:7; 1 Cor 1:2), is not just speculation on the part of the church, for she knows from experience that many times those who have departed to the next life have appeared on earth, giving assistance and encouragement to those still on earth. For a very early example, from the year AD 107, we have this account about what happened during the night after the martyrdom of St. Ignatius of Antioch, as recounted by some of his fellow Christians who had witnessed him being devoured by lions in the stadium in Rome:

> Having ourselves been eye-witnesses of these things, and having spent the whole night in tears within the house, and having entreated the Lord, with bended knees and much prayer, that He would give us weak men full assurance concerning the things which had happened, it came to pass, on our falling into a brief slumber, that some of us saw the blessed Ignatius suddenly standing by us and embracing us, while others beheld him again praying for us, and others still saw him dripping with sweat, as if he had just come from his great labor, and standing by the Lord. When,

---

2. Sophrony, *Wisdom from Mount Athos*, 60–61, emphasis added.

therefore, we had with great joy witnessed these things, and had compared our several visions together, we sang praise to God, the giver of all good things, and expressed our sense of the happiness of the holy martyr.

And now we have made known to you both the day and the time when these things happened, so that, assembling ourselves together according to the time of his martyrdom, *we may have fellowship with this champion and noble martyr of Christ*, who trod under foot the devil, and perfected the course which, out of love to Christ, he had desired.[3]

Through the twenty centuries of Christian history there have been a number of saints who have been especially active in making appearances after their deaths to people on earth. St. Nicholas of Myra (fourth century; Asia Minor) and St. Nectarios of Aegina (nineteenth and twentieth centuries; Greece) come quickly to mind. Another such saint is St. Spyridon of Cyprus (fourth century), whose incorrupt relics were transported to the island of Corfu in 1453. Several times since then he has saved the island from pestilence, famine, and invasion; each of these occasions is marked to this day by a triumphant procession with his relics in the streets of the capital city. The most recent of these miraculous interventions by St. Spyridon occurred on August 11, 1716, when he appeared to the invading Ottoman Turks; surrounded by a great host of angels and holding a flashing sword in his right hand, he drove them away from the island.

How do we grow in our communion with the saints? First of all, we get to know them by reading their Lives, which have been compiled by hagiographers in the church beginning in the early centuries of the Christian era. Then, we ask them for their prayers, and we sense their presence, especially by meditating before their icons. On the day of the veneration of any particular saint, we hear hymns written about them in church services, including requests for their intercession, and with references to miracles they have performed both during their earthly lives and after their repose in the Lord.

We also have special access to the presence of the saints through their relics, bits of which are made available to the faithful. Many miracles have been accomplished through the relics of the saints through the centuries, as many Orthodox (and Roman Catholic and Oriental Orthodox) Christians can attest.

---

3. Roberts and Donaldson, *Ante-Nicene Fathers*, 1:131 (emphasis added).

Part 6—Our Friends in Christ

Of all the saints, the one whom each Orthodox Christian naturally gets to know a lot about and shares a very special relationship with is his or her patronal saint, the one we share a name with and may be specifically named after. There naturally also will be an ongoing special relationship with the patronal saint of one's local parish—the saint after whom the parish is named. And there may be local saints, such as St. Alexis of Wilkes-Barre and St. Raphael of Brooklyn, whom we will naturally get to know quite well if we live in the area in which they lived and labored for the Lord.

Just as none of us comes into this world apart from other people, so none of us can grow in the spiritual life, in closeness to Christ, without the help of many others—especially all those who have faithfully passed on the doctrines and practices of the Christian Faith to each succeeding generation. Preeminently, these faithful stewards and witnesses are all the saints, both known and unknown, who continue to live in Christ in the next life. Let us always remember this "great cloud of witnesses," and strive to grow in vibrant, life-giving communion with them. For truly, "God is wondrous in His saints" (Ps 67:36 LXX).

24

On the Importance of Spiritual Fathers

Amir Azarvan

Developing a close relationship with an experienced spiritual guide has long been treated throughout the Christian East as a key aspect of one's spiritual growth. This trusted mentor goes by a variety of names—*abba* (used in many Semitic languages), *geron* (Greek), *starets* (Russian), elder and spiritual father (or their female equivalents) are among the most common.[1] In this brief chapter, I will explain how the very nature of spiritual progress implies the importance of seeking out an elder for guidance, while attempting to dispel misconceptions and concerns that some might have of spiritual parenthood.

The Title of "Father"

Let us first consider the claim that the title of "father" should be directed to God, alone. Many contemporary Christians insist that the practice of addressing elders and certain clerics as "father" stands in direct violation of v. 23:9 in St. Matthew's Gospel: "Do not call anyone on earth your father; for One is your Father, He who is in heaven."

However, a comprehensive reading of the Scriptures reveals that a broader use of this term is not necessarily condemned. St. Paul implicitly (or explicitly, if one relies on the New International Version's translation) refers to himself as father to the Corinthians: "For though you might have ten thousand instructors in Christ, yet you do not have many *fathers*; for in

---

1. For brevity's sake only, I will henceforth restrict myself to the masculine expressions of *elder* and *spiritual father*.

Christ Jesus I have *begotten* you through the gospel" (1 Cor 4:15, emphases added).[2] In Luke 16:24, Lazarus cries out to "Father Abraham," who in turn calls him "son" in the very next verse. It is the very context of Matthew 23:9, Fr. Peter Gilquist suggests, that unlocks the true meaning of this passage:

> In saying "call no man father," our Lord is contending with certain rabbis of His day who were using these specific titles to accomplish their own ends. And had these same apostate rabbis been using other titles like *reverend* and *pastor*, Jesus, it seems to me, would have said of these as well, "Call no one reverend or pastor." (emphasis in original)

Interestingly, even Norman Geisler and Thomas Howe, the Evangelical theologians who authored the voluminous handbook on Bible difficulties *When Critics Ask*, agree that

> the context of Jesus' statement indicates that he is referring to taking human beings as *infallible* spiritual masters, not that he is opposed to having *fallible* spiritual mentors . . . Showing *proper respect* to our spiritual leaders is one thing (cf. 1 Tim. 5:17), but giving them unquestioned obedience and reverence that is due only to God is another.[3]

And Geisler and Howe are certainly correct. The church has always recognized that one's ability to serve as an elder is conditioned upon whether his guidance is of benefit to his spiritual child's soul. There is a story from the desert fathers in which a monk solicits St. Poemen's advice on whether he should leave his *abba*, who for unspecified reasons was harming his spiritual health. Surprised that he even asked whether he ought to stay with him," St. Poemen counsels him to leave his abba, saying that "if you see your soul being harmed by something there is no need to ask what to do."[4] Similarly, a well-known contemporary elder points out that

> a disciple is devoted to Christ, never to the elder as a person. If the latter did not fulfill that role then the subordinate had, according

---

2. Two verses later (1 Cor 4:17), the apostle Paul explicitly refers to St. Timothy as his "beloved and faithful son in the Lord" (emphasis added).

3. Geisler and Howe, *When Critics Ask*, 356.

4. Ward, *Desert Fathers*, 102.

to monastic rules and tradition, the right to reject him and search for another suitable elder.[5]

Scriptural Basis for the Use of Spiritual Fathers

The Scriptures plainly sanction the practice of seeking advice from those who have entered "by the narrow gate" (Matt 7:13). St. John Cassian's commentary on two examples from the Old and New Testaments is worth quoting at length:

> In spite of having been called three times by God, [Samuel] went to the elder, Eli, and was instructed and guided by him about how he should answer God (cf. 1 Sam. 3:9–10). Although God called him personally, none the less He wanted Samuel to receive the guidance of the elder, so that by means of this example we too might be led to humility.
>
> When Christ Himself spoke to Paul and called him, He could have opened his eyes at once and made known to him the way of perfection; instead He sent him to Ananias and told him to learn from him the way of truth, saying: "Arise and go into the city, and there you will be told what you must do" (Acts 9:6). In this manner He teaches us to be guided by those who are advanced on the way, so that the vision rightly given to Paul should not be wrongly interpreted; otherwise it might lead later generations presumptuously to suppose that each individual must be initiated into the truth directly by God, as Paul was, and not by the fathers.[6]

Thus, even those who subscribe to the doctrine of *sola scriptura*[7] must come to terms with the reality that the Bible, itself, provides clear support for the ancient Christian tradition of spiritual parenthood.

The Familiar Logic of Seeking Spiritual Fathers

It is especially easy to understand the rationale for seeking counsel from a spiritual father when one appreciates the similarity between the "science"

---

5. Markides, *Mountain of Silence*, 171.
6. St. John Cassian, "On the Holy Fathers of Sketis and on Discrimination," 107.
7. This doctrine holds that the Bible is the exclusive authority for the faith and practice of the believer.

of spiritual growth and the earthly sciences. Regarding the latter, Fr. John Romanides asks:

> How does a student achieve his proper place in his scientific field? Doesn't he need someone to teach him the science he is studying? Is he only taught by books, or is he also taught by living scientists?[8]

This analogy certainly resonates with me. As a graduate student, my training—or my scholarly "askesis," to make the analogy clearer—involved and necessitated studying under academic "elders" from whom I learned the theories and methods used in my discipline. To reach the state of illumination, therefore, one should find "a spiritual father who has already attained to this state, who is inclined to teach you the method for acquiring the knowledge of God and who is willing to help you advance spiritually."[9]

Spiritual Discernment

To extend this analogy further, my academic mentors taught me to discern between good and bad approaches to academic research. Through their guidance, I have enhanced my ability to avoid discredited theories, common methodological pitfalls, and other scholarly evils. Similarly, there is a right way and a wrong way to maneuver in the spiritual realm, and a true elder helps us to distinguish between the two. I will never forget the story of a close friend who had just begun immersing himself in the spiritual life. While praying one evening, he felt enveloped by a light that grew in intensity. He was very excited about this, sincerely believing that he had already reached a milestone in his spiritual development. He was excited to share this story with his spiritual father. But, to his surprise, his elder was unimpressed—his face suggesting that he was familiar with such accounts—and he instructed him to simply ignore the experience. My friend learned that day that he had not yet learned how to discern between good and evil spiritual forces. So long as the latter persist in the world, employing one of their most potent weapons—appeals to our ego—there is always the chance that one will fall victim to what the fathers call *plani*, or spiritual delusion.[10] A year or so later, my friend discovered a passage in which

---

8. Romanides, *Patristic Theology*, 59.
9. Romanides, *Patristic Theology*, 60.
10. The following story illustrates the deceptive nature of forces that seek to lead us

recently canonized saint Elder Porphyrios seemed to speak directly to his experience, and it provides further testimony of the importance of studying the lives and teachings of the saints (see ch. 25):

> Your spiritual guide will teach you how to get into the right order for prayer, because if you don't get into the right order, there's a danger of your seeing the luciferic light, of living in delusion.[11]

He goes on to warn that

> the most dreadful delusion can be created by spiritual prayer . . . undoubtedly you will begin to see lights, but not the light of Christ, and undoubtedly you will experience a pseudo-joy. But in your outward life, in your relations with other people, you will be ever more aggressive and irascible, more quick-tempered and fretful. These are the signs of a person who is deluded.[12]

Were it not for the experience-derived wisdom of his spiritual father, my friend would have remained in his deluded state.

The Way of Humility

When pride comes, then comes shame; But with the humble is wisdom. (Prov 11:2)

The act of obedience to a true spiritual father is also important because it sets in motion a process culminating in the knowledge and vision of God, or *theosis* (see ch. 14). We may depict this multi-stage process in the following manner:

Obedience → Humility → Dispassion → Spiritual knowledge

Obedience is spoken of favorably in the Scriptures (e.g., see 2 Thess 3:14, and Phlm 1:21). St. Peter teaches thusly: "Likewise you younger people, submit yourselves to your elders" (1 Pet 5:5).[13] Obedience "cuts off our

---

astray: "The devil appeared to a monk disguised as an angel of light, and said to him, 'I am the angel Gabriel, and I have been sent to you.' But the monk said, 'Are you sure you weren't sent to someone else? I am not worthy to have an angel sent to me.' At that the devil vanished." Ward, *Desert Fathers*, 165.

11. Elder Porphyrios, *Wounded by Love*, 124.

12. Ibid., 125.

13. "Younger people" could be understood as including anyone who is "young" in the faith. St. Paul is not exclusively referring to physical children when he expresses "no

self-will,"[14] and thus enables those among us who sincerely wish to follow Christ to deny themselves (Luke 9:23; see also Phil 2:3).

St. Diadochos of Photiki hails obedience as "chief among the initiatory virtues" because it "engenders humility within us."[15] As imitators of Christ, we must also acquire this latter virtue (Matt 11:29). In the parable of the guests, Jesus teaches that "whoever exalts himself will be humbled, and he who humbles himself will be exalted" (Luke 14:11). He so loved humility, writes St. Diadochos, that he was "obedient to His father even to the cross and death."[16] How can the Christian, therefore, take up his own cross (Matt 16:24) without pursuing the way of humility?

With humility comes dispassion (*apatheia*)—or freedom from self-love,[17] which manifests itself in anger, greed, pride, and other destructive thoughts.[18] According to St. Hesychios, both humility and dispassion lead to spiritual knowledge, and "without them no one can see God."[19] This is perhaps best understood when we follow St. John Cassian and others in rendering *apatheia* as "purity of heart,"[20] and then reflect on the words of Jesus, himself: "Blessed are the pure in heart, for they shall see God" (Matt 5:8).

But it is not necessary to restrict oneself to religious sources in demonstrating the benefits of humility. Recent scientific research points to its positive effects.[21] For instance, it has been shown to strengthen relationships,[22] reduce death anxiety,[23] result in better health outcomes,[24] and enhance happiness.[25] Far from being a "slave-virtue," as Robert Ingersoll (the "great

---

greater joy than to hear that [his] children walk in truth" (3 John 1:4).

14. St. Hesychios the Priest, "On Watchfulness and Holiness," 167.
15. St. Diadochos of Photiki, "On Spiritual Knowledge," 265.
16. Ibid.
17. Ibid.
18. Ware, "Introduction," 24.
19. St. Hesychios the Priest, "On Watchfulness and Holiness," 174.
20. Palmer et al., glossary to *The Philokalia*, 1:359. Similarly, St. Theodoros refers to dispassion as "blessed purity." Theodoros the Great Ascetic, "Century of Spiritual Texts," 19.
21. For a brief summary, see Davis and Hook, "Measuring Humility."
22. E.g., see Peters et al., "Associations between Dispositional Humility," 155–61.
23. E.g., see Kesebir, "Quiet Ego Quiets Death Anxiety," 610–23.
24. E.g., see Krause, "Religious Involvement," 23–39.
25. E.g., see Zalewska and Zawadzka, "Can Humility Bring Happiness," 433–49.

agnostic") describes it,[26] humility actually *frees* us from many of the problems that consume us.

A Final Thought

While scriptural precedent and the experience of the fathers both point to the value of finding an elder, it is not always possible to do so, especially in countries (like my own) where Orthodox Christians form a tiny minority. Yet it should go without saying that the sincere and humble seeker of God should not despair, for he always has recourse to holy tradition, which has recorded the wisdom of many elders, not just one.

---

26. Ingersoll, "What Is Religion?," 80.

PART 7

The Life to Come

25

Dwelling in the Love of God: Heaven and Hell as Our Response to God's Love

Jonathan Resmini

FAITH IS NOT A collection of doctrinal statements and conciliar decrees, nor is it a blind adherence to a book—even a divinely inspired one. It is, instead, a lived experience of the presence of God in practice and the trust that one has in God as a result.[1] The experience of God is the experience of God's love; "for God is Love" (1 John 4:8). God's love is given to us indiscriminately—to the good and the evil, the just and the unjust (cf. Matt 5:45). The love of God for his creation is everywhere present and eternal:

> For I am persuaded that neither death nor life, nor angels nor principalities nor powers, nor things present nor things to come, nor height nor depth, nor any other created thing, shall be able to separate us from the love of God which is in Christ Jesus our Lord. (Rom 8:38–39)

According to the apostle, nothing "shall be able to separate us from the love of God." If God is love and his love is eternal, indiscriminate and inescapable, then it stands to reason that there is nowhere that God is not present.[2] Not even hell.

Heaven is not the place of God's love and hell the place devoid of God's presence. As was stated above, however, God is even found in hell. How is

---

1. About the Christian hope, the Orthodox Christian theologian and philosopher Christos Yannaras, writes, "We have to compromise with a modest agnosticism . . . We know nothing of life after death." Yannaras et al., *Meaning of Reality*, 9.

2. The Orthodox Prayer to the Holy Spirit begins: "Heavenly King, the Comforter, the Spirit of Truth, Who are everywhere present and filling all things . . ."

this possible? How could God be in hell? To answer these we will first have to answer the question: What *are* heaven and hell? In this brief chapter we will come to see that the notion of hell as a place of fiery torment and heaven a place of constant feasting are not to be taken literally, but rather figuratively. I will not present heaven and hell as realities that are off in some distant uncertain future, but as experiences of God's love, which human beings are called to actualize in the present—experiences that continue into eternity. Finally, I will emphasize our own uncertainty about the future, leaving God to his own affairs.

A Utopian View of Heaven and Hell

First, it must be stated that the Orthodox understand heaven and hell in many ways—none of which present them as literal places. The Orthodox believe that heaven and hell are relational realities, that is, they are reflections of the way in which the human being perceives the love of God—which is freely given to all.[3] Therefore, both heaven and hell are utopias, in the literal sense of the term.[4] If heaven and hell are not places, how are they understood by the Orthodox?

A Threefold Perspective of Heaven and Hell

There are three perspectives concerning heaven and hell, which I will discuss in this chapter: (1) Heaven or hell is the condition of our relationship to God in the age to come; (2) Heaven or hell is the manner in which human beings experience the intermediate state between death and resurrection to new life in eternity; (3) Heaven and hell reflect the way in which human beings exist in the present reality—actualizing either heaven or hell.

---

3. "According to these views, Hell and Paradise do not exist from God's perspective, only from man's point of view . . . Just as the sun rises now upon the righteous and the unrighteous, so then he will send His grace to everyone, to sinners as well as the just. Sinners, however, as they will not have acquired spiritual sight, will feel the caustic properties of the light. This will be their Hell . . . The problem facing us is not whether we will see God at the Second Coming, but whether God will be Light for us and not fire." Thus, heaven and hell are not places, but the experience or perception of the love of God. We will return to this understanding as we discuss the judgment of God. Vlachos, *Science of Spiritual Medicine*, 56–57.

4. The term derives from the Greel *ou* ("not") + *topos* ("place").

Heaven and Hell in Eternity

The Orthodox have little assurance concerning the age to come. They do, however, have a profound hope in the "resurrection from the dead and the life of the age to come," to quote from the Nicene Creed. Not much is known about this future life in eternity. The Scriptures are relatively silent about eternal life following the general resurrection. The only hint is found in the Gospel of John. During the farewell discourse the Evangelist writes:

> Jesus spoke these words, lifted up His eyes to heaven, and said: "Father, the hour has come. Glorify Your Son, that Your Son also may glorify You, as You have given Him authority over all flesh, that He should give eternal life to as many as You have given Him. And this is eternal life, that they may know You, the only true God, and Jesus Christ whom You have sent." (John 17:1–3)

According to this passage, eternal life is to know "God, and Jesus Christ whom [He has] sent."

Thus, eternal life is an eternal relationship with God in Jesus Christ. Jesus is "the way, the truth, and the life" (John 14:6) of all. Orthodox Christians believe that God will resurrect everyone from the dead on the day of judgment. Depending on the state of each person in this life, that resurrection will be to either the joy of the eternal kingdom, or to eternal condemnation. This eternal state, as we will see below, is not a result of God's punishment, but rather of our own perception of God's love. This is what Orthodox Christians believe about the age to come *after* the general resurrection. What happens after death, but *prior* to this resurrection?

Heaven and Hell as Intermediate States

As with the hope of the resurrection and the life of the age to come, little can be said definitively about the intermediate state of the soul—that is, the state of the soul after death and prior to the resurrection of the dead. There have been numerous attempts to offer theological opinions concerning the "journey" of the soul after death.[5] Orthodox Christians, with some consistency, describe this intermediate state as a foretaste of the life of the age to come. Depending on the manner in which the one lives one's life in

---

5. It goes beyond the scope of this article to address the multiform image of this intermediate state according to Orthodox theology. For a detailed presentation of a number of these perspectives, see Constas, "To Sleep, Perchance to Dream," 91–124.

the present age, the intermediate state will be either a foretaste of heaven or hell. It is clear that the human experience of God after death and eternal position are intimately connected to one's life in this age.

Heaven and Hell as the Experience of God's Love Here and Now

Orthodox Christians believe that heaven and hell are experienced in the present. They are experiences of God's love, which begin here and now. This means that we are capable of making the world around us either heaven or hell by the choices we make in the present age.

The choices we make with regards to love continue into the future and determine how we will experience eternity. If in life we choose to be selfish and unloving, our eternal state will be one of torment—but a torment of our own creation. Thus although the Orthodox speak of a judgment, in accordance with the Scriptures, they do not believe that God punishes anyone—nor, however, does he reward anyone.

God Does Not Punish Us, nor Does He Reward Us

From the Orthodox perspective, God does not punish us by sending us to hell; our choices determine our experience of God's love in life, after death, and into eternity. St. John of Damascus writes:

> And so we know, that God does not punish anyone in the future, but everyone makes themselves receptive to share in God. And so to share in God is a delight, while not sharing in Him is hell.[6]

Everything we do in this age makes us either receptive or unreceptive to the fullness of God's love, which will be given to everyone in the age to come. In this view, we can offer a profoundly different interpretation of the scriptural passages associated with the final judgment. God does not send the goats to the eternal fire anymore than he sends the sheep to the joy at his right hand (cf. Matt 25). He does not create a creature destined to eternal punishment. The Orthodox have characteristically understood scriptural passages that speak of God as punisher (e.g., Job 31:14) as figurative expressions of our perceptions of God's rejected love. As Fr. John Romanides put it, "God becomes an enemy and a punishing power only from the point of

---

6. Quoted in Sanidopoulos, "Saint John of Damascus on Hell."

view of those who by their will and perception stand in opposition to *God's love*."[7] We *choose* to be tormented by the love of God from this life into eternity. It is our choice to exist, or not to exist, as love that determines our present and future experience.[8]

Whereas some Christians think of heaven and hell respectively in terms of future bliss and punishment, the Orthodox always speak about both in terms of the present. The kingdom of God is within (cf. Luke 17:21). It is found in the heart of the believer. Hell, likewise, is a present reality that takes root within the hearts of those who live contrary to the love of God.

We Know Not Their Hearts

Orthodox Christians cannot assume that they will receive God's love as joy by virtue of their Orthodox faith. Nor can they assume that those who are not Christian (Orthodox or otherwise) will not receive the love of God as light, as opposed to fire.[9] We are not in it—the Christian life, that is—to avoid punishment or receive a reward. Neither are we Christians to mete out punishments or rewards to others. Orthodox Christians seek to fulfill the commandments of God, because that is what makes us authentically human. It is enough for us to love God with all our heart, soul, and mind, as well as our neighbors as ourselves (cf. Matt 22:37–40). We cannot know what the future state of anyone will be, for we do not know the inner hearts of others (cf. Rom 2). Orthodox Christians hope all will come to the knowledge of God and experience the love of God as heaven, but they acknowledge the human freedom to choose.

In summary, there is no locational difference between heaven and hell. They are not places, but rather our experience of God's love. We can

---

7. Romanides, *An Outline of Orthodox Patristic Dogmatics*, 99 (emphasis in original).

8. In Orthodox spirituality (as far as I understand it) everything is about cultivating, maintaining, and actualizing God's love as a state of being. Our free will is given to us to not only receive God's love, but to be infused with God's love. We are meant to become love because God is love. We manifest our free will only by our choice to exist as love; that is, to be in communion with God as love. God has given human beings a great deal of agency out of his great love for us. In doing so he freely limits his own omnipotence. He has given us the power to determine our own present and future state. Having been created from nothing we would naturally return to nothing. Instead he preserves us in his eternal love, which we choice either to actualize as our being (becoming "partakers of the divine nature") or fight against, thus creating our own eternal hell.

9. See Vlachos, *Science of Spiritual Medicine*, 57.

Part 7 — The Life to Come

live our eternal life in the kingdom of heaven, even in the present moment, if we choose to actualize the love of God. Heaven and hell are to dwell in the love of God, but how we experience this love is up to us.

Bibliography

Aghiorgoussis, Maximos. "The Unity of the Church: An Orthodox Point of View." *Greek Theological Review* 50 (2005) 141–85.
Alexander. *Father Arseny, 1893–1973: Priest, Prisoner, Spiritual Father*. Translated by Vera Bouteneff. Crestwood, NY: St. Vladimir's Seminary Press, 1998.
Alfeyev, Hilarion. *Orthodox Christianity*. Vol. 2, *Doctrine and Teaching of the Orthodox Church*. Crestwood, NY: St. Vladimir's Seminary Press, 2012.
Aslan, Reza. *Zealot: The Life and Times of Jesus of Nazareth*. New York: Random House, 2014.
"An Astronomer's Explanation for the Star of Bethlehem." *Science 2.0*. December 25, 2008. http://www.science20.com/news_articles/astronomers_explanation_star_bethlehem.
Augustine. *Contra Julianum Pelagianum* [Against Julian]. Translated by Matthew A. Schumacher. Fathers of the Church 35. Washington, DC: Catholic University of America Press, 1957.
———. *A Treatise on the Spirit and the Letter*. In Schaff, *Nicene and Post-Nicene Fathers*, 1st ser., 5:301–95.
Azarvan, Amir. "Are Highly Theistic Countries Dumber? Critiquing the Intelligence-Religiosity Nexus Theory." *Catholic Social Science Review* 18 (2013) 151–68.
Barker, William S. "Prayers: Carefully Written or Spontaneous." *Reformed Worship*. http://www.reformedworship.org/article/september-1986/prayers-carefully-written-or-spontaneous.
Barr, Stephen M. *Modern Physics and Ancient Faith*. Notre Dame: University of Notre Dame Press, 2006.
Basil. *Ascetical Works*. Translated by Ludwig Schopp. Fathers of the Church 9. Washington, DC: Catholic University of America Press, 1962.
———. *De Spiritu Sancto*. In Schaff, *Nicene and Post-Nicene Fathers*, 2nd ser., 8:138–250.
———. *On Social Justice*. Translated by C. Paul Schroeder. Crestwood, NY: St. Vladimir's Seminary Press, 2009.
Beauregard, Mario, et al. "Manifesto for a Post-Materialist Science." *Explore: The Journal of Science and Healing* 10 (2014) 272–74.

Bibliography

Becker, Sascha O., and Ludger Woessmann. "Knocking on Heaven's Door? Protestantism and Suicide." Warwick Economic Research Papers. University of Warwick, June 2011. http://www2.warwick.ac.uk/fac/soc/economics/research/workingpapers/2011/twerp_966.pdf.

Behr, John. *Irenaeus of Lyons: Identifying Christianity*. Oxford: Oxford University Press, 2013.

———. "A Note on the Ontology of Gender." *St. Vladimir's Theological Quarterly* 42 (1998) 363–72.

Behr-Sigel, Elisabeth. "The Ordination of Women: Also a Question for the Orthodox Churches." In *The Ordination of Women in the Orthodox Church*, edited by Elisabeth Behr-Sigel and Kallistos Ware, 11–48. Geneva: WCC Publications, 2000.

Bonner, Gerald. "Augustine's Theology on 'Adam.'" In *Augustinus-Lexicon*, edited by Cornelius Mayer, 1:82. Stuttgart: Schwabe, 1986.

Botros, G. B. "Competing for the Future: Adaptation and the Accommodation of Difference in Coptic Immigrant Churches." PhD diss., University of Toronto, 2005.

Bunyan, John. "I Will Pray with the Spirit, and with the Understanding Also." Edited by George Offor. *TruthinHeart.com*. Written 1662. http://truthinheart.com/EarlyOberlinCD/CD/Bunyan/text/Discourse.Touching.Prayer/Entire.Book.html.

———. *The Pilgrim's Progress*. Mineola, NY: Dover, 2003.

Calvin, John. *A Harmony of Matthew, Mark and Luke*. Edinburgh: St. Andrew's University Press, 1972.

The Canons of the Council in Trullo. In Schaff, *Nicene and Post-Nicene Fathers*, 2nd ser., 14:696–797.

Carlton, Clark. *The Way: What Every Protestant Should Know about the Orthodox Church*. Salisbury, MA: Regina Orthodox, 1997.

Cassian, John. "On the Holy Fathers of Sketis and on Discrimination." In Palmer et al., *Philokalia*, 1:94–108.

Chrysostom, John. *The Commentary on Galatians*. In Schaff, *Nicene and Post-Nicene Fathers*, ser. 1, 13:8–95.

———. *Homilies on Genesis 1–17*. Translated by Robert C. Hill. Fathers of the Church 74. Washington, DC: Catholic University of America Press, 1986.

———. *The Homilies on Paul's Epistle to the Romans*. In Schaff, *Nicene and Post-Nicene Fathers*, 1st ser., 11:604–997.

———. *Homilies on the Gospel of St. Matthew*. In Schaff, *Nicene and Post-Nicene Fathers*, ser. 1, 10:16–17.

———. *Homilies on Thessalonians*. In Schaff, *Nicene and Post-Nicene Fathers*, 1st ser., vol. 13.

———. "Homily 28 on Matthew." In Schaff, *Nicene and Post-Nicene Fathers*, 1st ser., 10:917–23.

———. *On Wealth and Poverty*. Translated by Catherine Roth. Crestwood, NY: St. Vladimir's Seminary Press, 1981.

———. *Treatise Concerning the Christian Priesthood*. In Schaff, *Nicene and Post-Nicene Fathers*, 1st ser., 9:37–122.

Clark Carlton. *The Way: What Every Protestant Should Know about the Orthodox Church*. Salisbury, MA: Regina, 1997.

Cohen-Zada, Danny, and William Sander. "Religious Participation versus Shopping: What Makes People Happier?" *Journal of Law and Economics* 54 (2011) 889–906.

Bibliography

Constas, Nicholas. "To Sleep, Perchance to Dream: The Middle State of Souls in Patristic and Byzantine Literature." *Dumbarton Oaks Papers* 55 (2001) 91–124.
Cyril of Alexandria. *Commentary on John*. In *The Faith of the Early Fathers*, vol. 3, edited and translated by William A. Jurgens. Collegeville: Liturgical, 1979.
Dallen, James. *Reconciling Community*. Collegeville: Pueblo, 1986.
Davis, Don Emerson, Jr., and Joshua N. Hook. "Measuring Humility and Its Positive Effects." *Observer* 26 (2013) n.p. http://www.psychologicalscience.org/index.php/publications/observer/2013/october-13/measuring-humility-and-its-positive-effects.html.
De Rose, Peter L., and Jane Garry. "Death or Departure of the Gods: Motif A192, and Return, Motif A193." In *Archetypes and Motifs in Folklore and Literature: A Handbook*, edited by Jane Garry and Hasan El-Shamy, 17–23. Armonk, NY: Sharpe, 2005.
Diadochos of Photiki. "On Spiritual Knowledge." In Palmer et al., *Philokalia*, 1:253–96.
"The Didache." In Staniforth, *Early Christian Writings*, 191–99.
The Divine Liturgy of St. John Chrysostom. http://www.orthodox.net/services/sluzebnic-chrysostom.pdf.
Douglas, A. Vibert. "Forty Minutes with Einstein." *Journal of the Royal Astronomical Society of Canada* 50 (1956) 99–102
Elder Porphyrios. *Wounded by Love: The Life and Wisdom of Elder Porphyrios*. Limni, Greece: Romiosyni, 2005.
Fagerberg, David W. *On Liturgical Asceticism*. Washington, DC: Catholic University of America Press, 2013.
FitzGerald, Kyriaki Karidonyanes. *Women Deacons in the Orthodox Church: Called to Holiness and Ministry*. Brookline, MA: Holy Cross Orthodox Press, 1999.
Fitzgerald, Thomas. "The Sacraments." *Greek Orthodox Archdiocese of America*. http://www.goarch.org/ourfaith/ourfaith7105.
Florovsky, Georges. *The Byzantine Ascetic and Spiritual Fathers*. Collected Works of Georges Florovsky 10. Vaduz, Liechtenstein: Büchervertriebsanstalt, 1987.
———. *Collected Works, Bible, Church, Tradition: An Eastern Orthodox View*. Belmont, MA: Nordland, 1972.
Gabriel, George S. *Mary: The Untrodden Portal of God*. Ridgewood, NJ: Zephyr, 2000.
Geisler, Norman, and Thomas Howe. *When Critics Ask: A Popular Handbook on Bible Difficulties*. Grand Rapids: Baker, 1992.
Gillquist, Peter. *Becoming Orthodox*. Nashville: Wolgemuth & Hyatt, 1989.
Gregory of Nyssa. *Concerning Almsgiving*. Translated by Richard McCambly. https://www.sage.edu/faculty/salomd/nyssa/benef.html.
Grisbrooke, W. Jardine, ed. *The Spiritual Counsels of Father John of Kronstadt*. Crestwood, NY: St. Vladimir's Seminary Press, 1981.
Harakas, Stanley S. *Toward the Transfigured life*. Minneapolis: Light & Life, 1983.
Harpham, Geoffrey. *The Ascetic Imperative in Culture and Criticism*. Chicago: University of Chicago Press, 1987.
Harrison, Nonna Verna. "Orthodox Arguments against the Ordination of Women as Priests." In Hopko, *Women and the Priesthood*, 165–87.
Hart, David Bentley. *The Experience of God: Being, Consciousness, Bliss*. New Haven: Yale University Press, 2013.
Heisenberg, Werner. *Across the Frontiers*. Translated by Peter Heath. New York: Harper & Row, 1974.

Bibliography

Hesychios the Priest. "On Watchfulness and Holiness." In Palmer et al., *Philokalia*, 1:162–98.

Hippolytus. *On the Apostolic Tradition*. Crestwood, NY: St. Vladimir's Seminary Press, 2001.

Höllinger, Franz, et al. "Christian Religion, Society and the State in the Modern World." *Innovation: The European Journal of Social Sciences* 20 (2007) 133–57.

Holy Apostles Convent. *The Life of the Virgin Mary, the Theotokos*. Buena Vista, CO: Holy Apostles Convent Publications, 1989.

Holy Transfiguration Monastery. *A Prayer Book for Orthodox Christians*. Boston: Holy Transfiguration Monastery, 1987.

Hopko, Thomas. "God and Gender: Articulating the Orthodox View." *St. Vladimir's Theological Quarterly* 37 (1993) 141–82.

———. "Presbyter/Bishop: A Masculine Ministry." In *Women and the Priesthood*, 139–64.

———, ed. *Women and the Priesthood*. Crestwood, NY: St. Vladimir's Seminary Press, 1999.

———. *Worship*. Vol. 2 of *The Orthodox Faith*. New York: Orthodox Church in America, 1983. http://oca.org/orthodoxy/the-orthodox-faith/worship.

Ignatius. "The Epistle to the Smyrnaeans." In Roberts and Donaldson, *Ante-Nicene Fathers*, 1:224–39.

———. "The Epistle to the Smyrnaeans." In Staniforth, *Early Christian Writings*, 101–5.

Ingersoll, Robert. "What Is Religion?" In *Atheism: A Reader*, edited by S. T. Joshi, 78–86. Amherst, NY: Prometheus, 2000.

Irenaeus. *Against Heresies*. In Roberts and Donaldson, *Ante-Nicene Fathers*, 1:841–1391.

John of Damascus. "Concerning the Holy and Immaculate Mysteries of the Lord." In Schaff, *Nicene and Post-Nicene Fathers*, 2nd ser., 9:736–41.

Josephus, Flavius. *Antiquities of the Jews: A History of the Jewish Peoples*. MacMay, 2008.

Justin Martyr. "First Apology." In *Early Christian Fathers*, edited by Cyril Richardson, 225–89. New York: Simon & Schuster, 1995.

Karras, Valerie. "Panel on Personhood: Medicine, Psychology, and Religion." In *Personhood: Orthodox Christianity and the Connection Between Body, Mind, and Soul*, edited by John Chirban, 101–2. Westport, CT: Bergin & Garvey, 1996.

Kesebir, Pelin. "A Quiet Ego Quiets Death Anxiety: Humility as an Existential Anxiety Buffer." *Journal of Personality and Social Psychology* 106 (2014) 610–23.

Kistler, Don, ed. *Sola Scriptura! The Protestant Position on the Bible*. Morgan, PA: Soli Deo Gloria, 1995.

Krause, Neal. "Religious Involvement, Humility, and Self-Rated Health." *Social Indicators Research* 98 (2010) 23–39.

Lightfoot, J. B., and J. R. Harmer, trans. *The Apostolic Fathers*. 2nd ed. Grand Rapids: Baker, 1989.

Lim, Chaeyoon. "In U.S., Churchgoers Boast Better Mood, Especially on Sundays." *Gallup*, March 22, 2012. http://www.gallup.com/poll/153374/churchgoers-boast-better-mood-especially-sundays.aspx.

Lindberg, Carter. *The European Reformations: Sourcebook*. Oxford: Blackwell, 2000.

Lossky, Vladimir. *In the Image and Likeness of God*. Crestwood, NY: St. Vladimir's Seminary Press, 1974.

———. *Orthodox Theology: An Introduction*. Crestwood, NY: St. Vladimir's Seminary Press, 2001.

Bibliography

Machen, J. Gresham. *New Testament Greek for Beginners*. 2nd ed. Upper Saddle River, NJ: Pearson / Prentice Hall, 2004.

MacMillan, Amanda. "People in Affluent Nations May Be More Depression-Prone." *CNN. com*. Posted July 26, 2011. http://www.cnn.com/2011/HEALTH/07/26/affluent.depression.prone.

Marius, Richard. *Martin Luther, the Christian between God and Death*. Cambridge: Belknap of Harvard University Press, 1999.

Markides, Kyriacos C. *Gifts of the Desert: The Forgotten Path of Christian Spirituality*. New York: Random House, 2005.

———. *Inner River: A Pilgrimage to the Heart of Christian Spirituality*. New York: Image, 2012.

———. *The Mountain of Silence: A Search for Orthodox Spirituality*. New York: Random House, 2001.

———. *Riding with the Lion: In Search of Mystical Christianity*. New York: Viking, 1995.

Mastrantonis, George. *Augsburg and Constantinople*. Brookline, MA: Holy Cross Orthodox Press, 1982.

Mathison, Keith A. *The Shape of Sola Scriptura*. Moscow, ID: Canon, 2001.

Matilda, Benita. "Rate of Depression on the Rise among Americans." *Science World Report*, October 1, 2004. http://www.scienceworldreport.com/articles/17533/20141001/rate-of-depression-among-americans-on-a-rise.htm.

Mavrogordatos, George. "Orthodoxy and Nationalism in the Greek Case." *West European Politics* 26 (2003) 117–36.

Maximus the Confessor. "Difficulty 41." In *Maximus the Confessor*, translated by Andrew Louth, 155–62. London: Routledge, 1996.

———. "Two Hundred Texts on Theology and the Incarnate Dispensation of the Son of God: Second Century." In Palmer et al., *Philokalia*, 2:137–63.

Meyendorff, John. *Byzantine Theology: Historical Trends and Doctrinal Themes*. New York: Fordham University Press, 1983.

Moevs, Christian. *The Metaphysics of Dante's Comedy*. Oxford: Oxford University Press, 2005.

Mother Mary. *The Festal Menaion*. London: Faber & Faber, 1977.

NASA. "Dark Energy, Dark Matter." National Aeronautics and Space Administration. http://science.nasa.gov/astrophysics/focus-areas/what-is-dark-energy.

Neusner, Jacob, trans. *The Babylonian Talmud: A Translation and Commentary*. Peabody: Hendrickson, 2005.

Nipperdey, T. "In Search of Identity: Romantic Nationalism, Its Intellectual, Political and Social Background." In *Romantic Nationalism in Europe*, edited by J. C. Eade, 1–15. Canberra, Australia: Australian National University, 1983.

O'Laughlin, Thomas. *Didache: A Window on the Earliest Christians*. Grand Rapids: Baker Academic, 2010.

Organ, Deborah A. "Immigrants and Inculturation." *America: The National Catholic Review*, November 10, 2003. http://americamagazine.org/issue/459/article/immigrants-and-inculturation.

Ouspensky, Leonid. *Theology of the Icon*. Vol. 1. Crestwood, NY: St. Vladimir's Seminary Press, 1978.

Palmer, G. E. H., et al., eds. *The Philokalia*. Vols. 1 & 2. London: Faber & Faber, 1979 & 1981.

Bibliography

Papageorgiou, Panayiotis. "Chrysostom and Augustine on the Sin of Adam and Its Consequences." *St. Vladimir's Theological Quarterly* 39 (1995) 361–78.

Patsavos, Lewis. "The Canonical Tradition of the Orthodox Church." Greek Orthodox Archdiocese of America. http://www.goarch.org/ourfaith/ourfaith7071.

Pelikan, Jaroslav J., and Helmut Lehmann. *Luther's Works*. American ed. St. Louis: Concordia / Fortress, 1962.

Penrose, Roger. *The Emperor's New Mind*. Oxford University Press, 1989.

Peters, Annette, et al. "Associations between Dispositional Humility and Social Relationship Quality." *Psychology* 2 (2011) 155–61.

A Pocket Prayer Book for Orthodox Christians. Englewood, NJ: Antiochian Orthodox Christian Archdiocese of North America, 1980.

Quasten, Johannes, and Walter Burghardt, eds. *The Letter of St. Cyprian of Carthage*. Translated by G. W. Clarke. New York: Newman, 1984.

Roberts, Alexander, and James Donaldson, eds. *Ante-Nicene Fathers*. Vol. 1. Grand Rapids: Eerdmans, 1981.

Romanides, John. *An Outline of Orthodox Patristic Dogmatics*. Rollinsford, NH: Orthodox Research Institute, 2004.

Romanides, John. *Patristic Theology: The University Lectures of Fr. John Romanides*. Hong Kong: Uncut Mountain, 2008.

Routledge, Clay. "Are Religious People Happier than Non-Religious People?" *Psychology Today*, December 5, 2012. https://www.psychologytoday.com/blog/more-mortal/201212/are-religious-people-happier-non-religious-people.

Sanidopoulos, John. "Saint John of Damascus on Hell." *Mystagogy* (blog). http://www.johnsanidopoulos.com/2013/12/saint-john-of-damascus-on-hell.html.

Schäfer, Peter. *Jesus in the Talmud*. Princeton: Princeton University Press, 2007.

Schaff, Philip, ed. *The Creeds of Christendom with a History and Critical Notes*. Vol. 3. Grand Rapids: Baker, 1993.

———. *Nicene and Post-Nicene Fathers*. 1st and 2nd series. Grand Rapids: Eerdmans, 2009.

Schmemann, Alexander. *The Eucharist: Sacrament of the Kingdom*. Crestwood, NY: St. Vladimir's Seminary Press, 1987.

Shanbour, Michael. "The Sacrament of Confession." Saints Peter and Paul Antiochian Orthodox Christian Church. http://www.peterandpaul.net/art-confession.

Smart, J. J. C., and J. J. Haldane. *Atheism and Theism*. 2nd ed. Oxford: Blackwell, 2003.

Sophrony, Archimandrite. *Wisdom from Mount Athos*. Crestwood, NY: St. Vladimir's Seminary Press, 1975.

Spitzer, Robert J. *New Proofs for the Existence of God*. Grand Rapids: Eerdmans, 2010.

Sproul, R. C. "The Establishment of Scripture." In Kistler, *Sola Scriptura*, 39–58.

Stade, C., trans. *The Explanation by Blessed Theophylact of the Holy Gospel, according to St. Matthew*. House Springs, MO: Chrysostom, 1992.

Staniforth, Maxwell, trans. *Early Christian Writings*. London: Penguin, 1987.

Stokoe, Mark, et al. "The Alaskan Mission (1794–1870)." Chapter 1 of *Orthodox Christians in North America (1794–1994)*, edited by Mark Stokoe and Leonid Kishkovsky. http://oca.org/history-archives/orthodox-Christians-na/chapter-1.

Stylianopoulos, Theodore. "How Are We Saved?" Greek Orthodox Archdiocese of America. November 2, 2012. http://www.goarch.org/ourfaith/how-are-we-saved.

———. *The New Testament: An Orthodox Perspective*. Vol. 1, *Scripture, Tradition, Hermeneutics*. Brookline, MA: Holy Cross Orthodox Press, 1997.

Bibliography

Suetonius. "Divus Claudius." In *The Twelve Caesars*, edited by James Rives, 178–206. London: Penguin Classics, 2007.

Syncellus, George. *The Chronography of George Synkellos: A Byzantine Chronicle of Universal History from the Creation*. Translated by William Adler and Paul Tuffin. Oxford: Oxford University Press, 2002.

Tacitus. *Annals*. Translated by Cynthia Damon. London: Penguin Classics, 2013.

Thalassios. "On Love, Self-Control and Life in Accordance with the Intellect: Third Century." In Palmer et al., *Philokalia*, 2:319–24.

Theodoros the Great Ascetic. "A Century of Spiritual Texts." In Palmer et al., *Philokalia*, 2:14–37.

Theophan the Recluse. "The Fruits of Prayer." In Ware, *Art of Prayer*, 124–63.

Topping, Eva. *Holy Mothers of Orthodoxy*. Minneapolis: Light & Life, 1987.

Torgler, Benno, and Christoph A. Schaltegger. "New Evidence on Differences between Protestantism and Catholicism." *Journal for the Scientific Study of Religion* 53 (2014) 316–40.

Tsang, Jo-Ann, et al. "Why Are Materialists Less Happy? The Role of Gratitude and Need Satisfaction between Materialism and Life Satisfaction." *Personality and Individual Differences* 64 (2014) 62–66.

Tserkov, Russkaia Pravoslavnaia. *Great Book of Needs*. Waymart, PA: St. Tikhon's Seminary Press, 1998.

Valantasis, Richard. *The Making of the Self*. Eugene, OR: Cascade, 2008.

Vincent of Lérins. *The Fathers of the Church*. Vol. 7. Translated by Rudolph Morris. Washington, DC: Catholic University of America Press, 1949.

Vlachos, Hierotheos. *Empirical Dogmatics of the Orthodox Catholic Church: According to the Spoken Teaching of Father John Romanides*. Vols. 1 and 2. Translated by Pelagia Selfe. Levadia, Greece: Birth of the Theotokos Monastery, 2013.

———. *The Science of Spiritual Medicine: Orthodox Psychotherapy in Action*. Levadia, Greece: Birth of the Theotokos Monastery, 2010.

Ward, Benedicta. *The Desert Fathers: Sayings of the Early Christian Monks*. London: Penguin, 2003.

Ware, Kallistos. Foreword to Yannaris, *Freedom of Morality*.

———. *The Orthodox Way*. Crestwood, NY: St. Vladimir's Seminary Press, 1995.

———. "The Way of the Ascetics: Negative or Affirmative?" In *Asceticism*, edited by Vincent L. Wimbush and Richard Valantasis, 3–15. New York: Oxford University Press.

Ware, Timothy. Introduction to *The Art of Prayer: An Orthodox Anthology*. London: Faber & Faber, 1997.

———. *The Orthodox Church*. London: Penguin, 1963.

Weyl, Hermann. *The Open World: Three Lectures on the Metaphysical Implications of Science*. New Haven: Yale University Press, 1932.

White, James. "Sola Scriptura and the Early Church." In Kistler, *Sola Scriptura*, 27–62.

Whiteford, John. "Responses to Protestant Apologists on Sola Scriptura." St. Jonah Orthodox Church. http://www.saintjonah.org/articles/responses_sola.htm.

Wiles, Maurice. *The Making of Christian Doctrine*. Cambridge: Cambridge University Press, 1967.

Williams, Raymond B. *Christian Pluralism in the United States: The Indian Immigrant Experience*. Cambridge: Cambridge University Press, 1996.

Bibliography

Wolgemuth, Charles W. "Trend: Does Cell Biology Need Physicists?" *Physics* 4 (2011). https://physics.aps.org/articles/v4/4.

Woloschak, G. E. "The Compatibility of the Principles of Evolution with Eastern Orthodoxy." *St. Vladimir's Theological Quarterly* 55 (2011) 209–31.

Yannaras, Christos. *The Freedom of Morality*. Crestwood, NY: St. Vladamir's Seminary Press, 1984.

Yannaras, Christos, et al. *The Meaning of Reality: Essays on Existence and Communion, Eros and History*. Los Angeles: Sebastian, 2011.

Zalewska, Justyna, and Anna Maria Zawadzka. "Can Humility Bring Happiness in Life? The Relationship between Life Aspirations, Subjective Well-Being, and Humility." *Annals of Psychology (Roczniki Psychologiczne)* 16 (2013) 433–49.

Zizioulas, John D. *Being as Communion: Studies in Personhood and the Church*. Crestwood, NY: St. Vladimir's Seminary Press, 1985.

———. *The Eucharistic Communion and the World*. Edited by Luke Ben Tallon. New York: T. & T. Clark International, 2011.

www.ingramcontent.com/pod-product-compliance
Lightning Source LLC
Chambersburg PA
CBHW051736230426
43670CB00012B/2049